MW01099099

# TABLE OF CONTENTS

# Fenny to Fran

## Reflections on Growing

FRAN VANDERPOL

One Printers Way
Altona, MB R0G 0B0
Canada

www.friesenpress.com


First Edition — 2022



ISBN
978-1-03-910958-2 (Hardcover)
978-1-03-910957-5 (Paperback)
978-1-03-910959- (eBook)

*1. RELIGION, CHRISTIAN LIFE, PERSONAL MEMOIRS*

Distributed to the trade by The Ingram Book Company

Dedicated to the two people who
gave me life and
taught me how to live:

Siena Harsevoort-Hutten
and
Berend Jan (BJ) Harsevoort

"Whoever dwells in the shelter of the Most High
will rest in the shadow of the Almighty"
Bible, Psalm 91:1

*Wedding photos July 12, 1940. Plain people got married in black..*

*She was allowed light coloured stockings for this special occasion.*

# VIEWPOINT

When I drive through the mountain passes here in my beautiful British Columbia, it's a pleasure to pull over at a lofty viewpoint to look back at the road my husband, Pieter, and I are travelling. I want to see where we started, what we journeyed through, and how far we have come. Way back in the distance, at the bottom, I see the cultivated valley, with its fenced fields and straight rows of crops, tidy houses lining the streets. From this distance, it looks quite cozy. Then, we entered vast expanses of forests where my eyes were always alert for its wonders—eagles, or moose, or mountain goats—as well as its dangers. I was very thankful for paved roads, strong guardrails and clear road signs while navigating the twists, turns, and climbs.

I pause and take deep breaths, shaking out my muscles and joints to get the blood flowing again. I snap some photos and celebrate how far I've come and all the reality I've just travelled through. From a distant vantage point, it looks beautiful. However, I remember that there were also rough roads, hairpin bends, potholes and rocks on the road, traffic snarls, and long, slow climbs behind a line of trucks. Pine beetle infested forests, rockslides, or animal carcasses near the road speak of the hardships and tragedies. From my vantage point, I may still see storm clouds dumping their load here and there or remnants of huge snow banks. On my journey, there were breathtaking experiences, exciting memorable moments, risky incidents, and long, monotonous stretches; but mostly, there were the many miles of just driving along companionably. It's all part of the story.

We intend to get back in the car, merge into traffic, and continue around the next bend, anticipating what's ahead. I know the general direction we plan to travel, and I have a purpose, a destination, and a timeline in mind. But I don't really know what's going to happen until I experience it, kilometre by kilometre.

Having reached my seventies, I am taking some time to rest at a convenient viewpoint after my journey. It's also 2020. My chosen viewpoint coincides with a major disruption, as massive recovery work is suddenly needed to deal with a metaphorical global earthquake. Weeks after we celebrated my seventieth birthday, our province, along with much of the world, went into lockdown due to the COVID-19 global pandemic After a brief partial lifting of restrictions during the summer, we entered a second lockdown in early November, which took us through the winter and well into spring. The second summer was a bit more relaxed, thanks to the gift of vaccines, but we are still not out of the woods yet, trying very hard to come out of the fourth wave.

Added to this stress, our beloved Fraser Valley is struggling with the disastrous effects of an extra-ordinarily large rainfall, an atmospheric river that dropped up to 200 mm of water across southwestern BC in two days. While our home was safe, we, along with our city, province and country watched in horror. Whole towns needed to evacuate as they became unsafe. Close to home, the entire Sumas Prairie was under water. What had originally been Sumas Lake returned to its farthest shores. So many farms were flooded out, animals in distress or dead and infrastructure damaged and destroyed. Thankfully there was no loss of life here in our valley but the emotional stress and physical exhaustion take their toll. We are, at the time I am writing this, still mostly cut off by road and rail from the rest of BC and Canada as all of the major highways received extensive damage from flooding and landslides. It will take many months, if not longer, before things are back to 'normal'. So thankful for good leaders and for the strong and generous hearts, backs, minds and hands that dropped everything and gave their all.

My life was suddenly forced into a much slower pace, as did all of our lives around the globe. So, as I'm looking back over the road I have travelled, I'm also watching the massive efforts of various work crews dealing with the trauma, assessing the damage, and figuring out how to get traffic moving again.

The anxieties of dealing with a global pandemic and a climate catastrophe made us painfully aware of the cracks and weaknesses of the systems, beliefs and attitudes we had taken for granted. We also suddenly knew and recognized who were the real essential workers and what was most important in our lives, both personally and as a society. We know that surviving this pandemic, and the more frequent and more severe climate crisis will require an unprecedented level of global cooperation. Everything—business, education, politics, religion—has to pivot on a dime, providing opportunity and motivation to rethink and rebuild a better world.

During the pandemic, I had even more time on my hands. Social and casual interactions ground to a halt, essential meetings went online with Zoom, and I had long days and nights hunkered down in my home. So, the combination of having more time and lots to think about drove me to my keyboard to try to make a bit of sense of it all by looking at what I know: my story.

I look back over a full and rich life. With the perspective of time and distance, I recapture the places and people that are such precious and treasured memories. My eyes search out the patterns and themes—how the one scene connects and flows into the other. I want to drink it in thirstily, with new and much greater appreciation for each part. I want to "get the lay of the land" as I take some deep breaths and feel the sun on my face and the wind at my back. I want to celebrate life. My life. Your life. Everyone's life. Our world and our history consist of stories just like yours and mine. It's about real people, lives lived, dreams pursued, obstacles overcome, and identities more clearly discovered and defined.

When I feel rejuvenated and refreshed, and when the roads have been opened again, I intend to resume the journey and find out what's around the bend and over the next hill. There may yet be many roads to travel, mountains to climb, and new vistas yet to enjoy. I hope to be able to experience a lot more. I also hope that, having stopped at this Viewpoint, my eyes, ears, and heart will be more attuned to, and ready for, the upcoming adventures. I am excitedly looking forward to the future. My past, the road I have travelled, taught me valuable lessons and shaped me into the person I am. Now I want to continue to build on my life's experiences and lessons with renewed confidence.

My story is my legacy. It is particular to me. You have your own story, unique and important to you and the world you find yourself in. As you read my story, I hope that you are inspired to take time to stop at your life's viewpoints. They will look different from mine, but they will help you better see and understand your environment and your characteristic responses.

First of all, I want to capture my story to pass on to my children and grandchildren, my nieces and nephews, and anyone else that cares to spend a few hours with these pages. I hope to preserve some family history and give evidence to our shared humanity. It will include a recounting of details or, more accurately, mostly my own memories of events and the people that were a big part of them. That's a relatively straightforward and pleasant experience for the most part, largely because I have led a fairly safe and secure life. But it's so much more than a description of events, people, and places. Each memory is shaped and coloured by my perceptions and my emotional and spiritual awareness. This is my story, from my viewpoint, as a child, a teen, an adult, and a senior with time on her hands to reflect. Mostly, it's the seventy-year-old me trying to find the themes, patterns, truths, and growth that I have experienced during those years.

The writing experience has been therapeutic. I experienced, and re-experienced, so many emotions as I relived these moments. Some pages were written with tears flowing; for example, I wept again at my mother's deathbed. Other days, I was awash in regrets and guilt. Yet, the overwhelming emotion was gratitude. My family, parents, and siblings have always been an important part of my life, yet I take the people closest to me for granted. They are just there. It's when I stand at a viewpoint and see what they have always quietly been for me that my heart overflows. My husband, Pieter, and each one of our children and grandchildren are precious gifts that have taught me so much about love, life and relationships. We have journeyed together for almost forty years now.

Other times, there were *Aha!* moments as I saw patterns of responses and behaviours that helped me understand my own unique character. I was able to see development and maturing, learning and growth. It helped me to be better aware of, and begin to address, some of my doubts and insecurities. If any of this resonates with you, helping you process your own experiences, that will be another win for writing these chapters.

It is my hope that you, dear reader, may be comforted and inspired by the truth that life is messy and complicated. We are all doing the best we can in our circumstances, unable to see a clear path ahead of us, yet taking one step at a time, sometimes with varying degrees of confidence, and other times with great hesitance and apprehension. Looking back, we see that life is not a manicured garden. It's a wilderness. An untamed forest.

Yet, I have experienced a presence, unseen but very real, that has been beside me, before me, and behind me every moment. In my baptism, it was promised and sealed to me that I belonged to God, and nothing could ever change that. God is and remains faithful. It was my journey to learn to know and walk with God. Many times, I did this consciously, or at least as well as I understood it. But, when I look back from the various viewpoints in my life, I am always amazed at just how closely and intentionally God was, and is, there in every detail. I see God around me, and more and more, I see how God has always been within me. My very being comes from, and is all interconnected with, God. As I follow the way of Christ, boldly taking on the name Christian—or "little Christ"—then I am also in God, synchronized, acting in rhythm as one. God is Love. So, I could also say that *Love* was, and is, there in every detail. I see Love around me and, increasingly, inside me. My very being comes from, and is all interconnected with, Love.

# HOLLAND

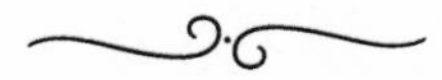

# CHAPTER 1

## Heemse

I am the fifth child of Siena Harsevoort-Hutten and Berend Jan Harsevoort. Eight-year-old Grace, six-year-old Harry, four-year-old Herman, and two-year-old Benny welcomed me into the flat I was born in above Oostenbrink's Furniture Store in Heemse Overijsel, the Netherlands. In harmony with the traditions, being the second daughter, I was given the name Fennigje, in honour of Opoe, my Mom's mother. Grace had been named after Dad's mother.

I read an interesting story about the history of this name in a book my cousin Fenny DeHeus had written in Holland called Everdina Johanna. The original Fennigien was a second wife to my great-great grandfather Frederik Breukelman and a stepmother to his children. Fennegien, at the age of thirteen suffered the trauma of losing both of her parents. She, and her sister and brother were sudden orphans. In 1847 Fennegien's name was recorded in the List of the Poor, the same year that her sister married and moved far away. She had been made a ward of the state at age nineteen and written in as epileptic insane. She wasn't extremely mentally ill or she would have been incarcerated rather than put under the care of the deacons. Also, the term insane covered a very wide range from being somewhat slower to learn to being seriously disturbed. There were no treatments or medications and anyone who was 'different' was quickly labeled as insane.

She must have learned to live and function despite her handicaps, otherwise Frederik would not have asked her to marry him and care for his children, and the church would not have allowed it. For twelve years they were a family. It was obvious that Gerrit, the oldest son of Frederik, had bonded with his stepmother Fennegien because he named his fifth child and third daughter after her. That third daughter was my Opoe, Fennigje Breukelman. I, and many of her granddaughters carry on her name.

Fennigje was born two months premature on Sept. 26, 1893. She was extremely tiny and fragile, too weak even to cry. They wrapped her in warm cloths and laid her in her cradle with warm stones to keep her at the correct temperature. This vulnerable baby survived the first scary years. She suffered all the childhood diseases and took longer to recover. When she reached school age this tiny girl determinedly made the long daily trek walking to school with her siblings and neighbourhood children.

When tall, outgoing Jan Harm Hutten caught her eye, and she his, and they wanted to get married it must have caused some concern for her parents. Would she, who had been born tiny and premature, who had suffered many serious illnesses as a child, be able to handle all the rigours of marriage and family? She barely reached his shoulders. Nevertheless they did get married and that tiny, spunky Fennigje bore nine children who all lived and thrived. She worked very hard to keep the family and the farm going and lived to be eighty-two.

*Opoe Fenny feeding her chickens*

Herman was staying with this Opoe and Opa, and Mom's younger siblings during my birth. His memory is that when Opoe told him he had a baby sister, Uncle John told him not to believe her. So, he didn't believe it until he could no longer deny my existence when he returned home. Of course, I have no memories of the events or the place, but I like to imagine them fighting to hold me and take me for walks in the pram. It was a time in which children were not to be spoiled. Knowing my siblings, however, I'm sure they would have been good to me.

*Grace, Ben, Herman and Harry. This is maybe their reaction when they first met me.*

We were part of a large extended family that all lived nearby. My Mom was the third of nine children, and my Dad was the fourth of five, so there were many Ooms and Tantes (aunts and uncles) and cousins to get to know. However, it would be many years before I actually started getting to know most of them.

My Dad's family were farmers. They owned their farm. It wasn't an extremely large or prosperous farm, but it provided for their needs. And it rooted them in place, geographically and socially. They were landowners.

*Oma and Opa Harsevoort*

*Opa Harsevoort*

*Oma Harsevoort*

*Dad's family: Albertus, Oma, Dad, Opa and Gerrit Jan (GJ). His two sisters, Hendrikje and Zwaantje, were already married so not in the photo.*

*This stone was above the door to the old house my Opa and Dad were born in. It reads "Fear God and keep his commandments for this is the whole duty of man." Ecclesiastes 12:13*

My Mom's family were farmers as well. However, they rented their land. Thus, their struggle to provide for their family was more challenging. A flock of chickens, a few milk cows, a pen full of pigs, some feed crops, and a large kitchen garden kept the whole family busy and allowed them a meagre living. They didn't have the roots, security, or the social status of land ownership. So, when Dad first started courting my Mom, his father was not pleased. Nevertheless, Dad persisted. He had met the most beautiful woman, and he wanted to go through life with her.

*Opa and Opoe Hutten*

*Opoe and Opa Hutten. I had to include this one!*

*Mom's family. Mom is second from the right in the back row.*

Both families were well aware of their place in the social structure of the time, which was also played out within the church. Within a community, the top class consisted of the Mayor, the Dominee (Pastor), the School Master, other professionals, and the richest farmers. They were accorded every respect. Then, it was layered into many subtle, but well-respected strata. Everyone knew their place, even where to sit in church, and few sought to go outside of their class. It was especially difficult for my mother to get beyond this, for she always remained very humble and showed a healthy respect and deference for people in positions of authority and greater wealth.

This is the world I was born into. It was not too different from the world my parents grew up in, and even the one my grandparents grew up in. Change had happened over the past centuries, but it was gradual enough that the generations could understand and relate to one another. All my ancestors, going back more than two hundred years, had been born and lived within less than thirty kilometres of where I was born. It is likely that none of them had ventured very far from this area during their lives. This was all about to change!

*Family photos taken before we left.*

*Grace was 10, Harry 7, Herman 6, Benny 3 and me 16 months.*

# CANADA

# THE FIRST DECADE

*The farewell! Oom Bats bringing us to the train in the horse-drawn carriage while Mom's sisters, Annichien, Dien, and Fenna, wave us off.*

*The Volendam, our transportation to our new home. Mom, Grace, Herman, Benny and I slept in one area and Dad and Harry slept in the men's area.*

# CHAPTER 2

## Immigration (June 1951)

Sixteen months after I was born, we were onboard a repurposed troop ship on our way to a land far away and unknown. Two Opas, one Opoe, and many Ooms, Tantes, and cousins were left behind — in their and my parents' minds, never to see each other again. My Mom's brother, Oom Gerrit, and his wife, Tante Janke (pronounced Yanka), had immigrated the year before and were "settled" in an old white frame house in Aldershot, a suburb of Burlington, Ontario. After a week-long ocean voyage to land in Quebec City, we took a train to Hamilton, where Oom Gerrit and Tante Janke met us. We would live with them for about sixteen months until we could get a place of our own. How brave my parents, uncle, and aunt were!

When we asked Dad why they immigrated, he said that there were a number of factors. Holland was in a very difficult state after the economic depression and subsequent occupation during the war. Severe housing shortages, a black market, out-dated economic and agriculture systems, a fairly rigid social system, and the impending threat of socialism and communism made emigrating a viable option to consider. Many Dutch citizens were thinking and talking about it. "Emigrating was in the air," he would say, as many families considered it and more and more were making plans. Envisioning a future for their five young children, they considered which country would provide the better opportunities.

The Dutch Premier Drees, and even the beloved Queen Juliana, were encouraging their citizens to consider emigrating. Canada needed farm workers—the need was even greater after losing so many of its young men during the war. The Dutch loved Canadians. They still do. The Canadians had played a significant part in liberating Holland from the Germans, sacrificing many young lives in the process. So, Holland's surplus of farm workers became the new citizens and farmers in a growing and developing country. It seemed like a very good solution.

My cousin Fenny DeHeus, in her book, titled *Everdina Johanna*, writes that, besides leaving an overcrowded Netherlands with high unemployment and a critical housing shortage in the hopes of more opportunities and a better future, there were also faith considerations. In 1944, in some of the darkest days of the war, there had been a very painful split in the church that both my father and mother's families were a part of. My mother's parents and some of her siblings remained in the original church, while many of the others, including my parents, joined the "liberated church." This caused considerable friction and pain within the family, though, thankfully, it did not break the close relationships. So, added to the economic opportunities was also the "call" to establish a faithful church in the new world. These two motivations became the focus and heart of how I remember my childhood.

My Mom's first visit back home occurred in 1963, to celebrate the fiftieth wedding anniversary of her parents. Our whole family went to the Toronto Airport to wave her off as she walked across the tarmac to climb the stairs into the airplane. Her family and friends eagerly listened to her stories of life in Canada. At one point, one of her family members said, "Now I think I know why you went to Canada. You talk so much about the church and the church community there. It sounds to me like you went to build a new church community." There was truth in this observation, but her words primarily reflected the importance of the church community in our lives.

My Dad and his brother—Oom GJ, we called him—promised each other that they would stay connected by regularly writing letters. Every week, Dad would sit down at his typewriter, a well-worn sheet of carbon paper between the two white pages, and faithfully chronicle the events and thoughts of the week. The letters contained family stories, church stories, and a summary of Sunday's sermon, I'm sure. Back in Heemse, his brother would do the same. They were as familiar with what was happening in the other's mind and life as if they lived in the same house. After many years, they decided to reduce the frequency to every other week, to allow time for the letters to pass in the mail. Moreover, with growing families and more involvement in church leadership, life became busier. They continued this exchange their whole lives. When Oom GJ was no longer able to write, his son Roelf took over, even after Oom GJ's death. Roelf continued to correspond with Dad until Dad died. Even when Dad was living in long-term care at Shalom Manor, without much happening in his life anymore, he always had a sheet of paper, with the carbon copy behind it, in his typewriter on his desk. Each day, he would type something, even if it were only a sentence or two. As family members would visit, they might chronicle their visit on his letter, and it would regularly get sent off to Holland. He had many binders full of the carbon copies he had saved over the years, many of them so faint they were barely legible. Unfortunately, he decided to get rid of them at some point, so I don't have the benefit of that living history to enhance my memories.

# CHAPTER 3

## Hannon (1952 to 1961)

We had arrived in Aldershot (Burlington) at the end of June 1951. Mom's brother, my Oom Gerrit, and his wife, Tante Janke (Yanka), had immigrated to Canada in 1950 and were living on the Gallagher farm in Aldershot. We moved in with them until we could get established. We stayed there for sixteen months.

*Our first home on Gallagher Rd. This picture was taken after we had moved. That's Uncle Gerry, Tante Janke and my cousin Grace and the old Studebaker.*

Due to a cash shortage in the Netherlands, each immigrant was allowed to take only one hundred dollars in cash per person. For us, that was seven hundred dollars. This meagre beginning had to be carefully rationed and supplemented by many hours of hard work at a labourer's wage. Sharing housing with my uncle and aunt helped both families.

Immigrants were allowed to take as many material goods as they had. So, my entrepreneurial father took a house along. They had owned a house in Holland but never actually lived in it. Due to the acute housing shortage, you could not ask renters to leave, so my parents ended up in that flat above Oostenbrink's store, where I was born. When they decided to emigrate, they sold their house and bought many of the pieces needed to build a new home. Doors, windows, and I don't know what all were packed, piece-by-piece, into a wooden crate and shipped to Hamilton.

As soon as he had earned a few dollars in this "land of opportunity," Dad purchased a lot on the other side of Hamilton, out in Hannon (right on Highway 53, just east of Mount Albion Road), for three hundred dollars. When the container arrived on the property, he began building the house.

During the day, he worked for Mr. Richardson, a building contractor in Aldershot. Then, he would take his old Model A Ford "up the mountain" to the rural community of Hannon to work all by himself until dark. Then, he would make the long trek back to Aldershot to begin all over the next morning. On a few occasions, on a Friday afternoon, Mr. Richardson would say to his crew, "We're going up to Ben's house," and they would all go and help Dad build. Saturdays, I'm sure, were also spent working on the house, but Sundays was a much needed and honoured day of rest and worship.

No wonder we moved into the shell of the house long before it was done, sixteen months after we landed. By that time, I was no longer the youngest. Little Johnny had joined the family, becoming the first of the three "*Canadezen*" (Canadian-born children). My sister, Grace, remembers that he would be left to sleep in the car on sunny days because it was warmer than the house.

The house was framed in, the outside walls covered with TenTest and the inside walls covered with cardboard that Dad had saved up for some time from grocery store and other boxes. It was insulated with newspapers and whatever else could be found. Inside there was minimal partitioning. The house was heated with a coal stove that was also the cooking stove. A long extension cord from our neighbours, the Spurrs, provided some basic light until we were connected to the grid. It was extremely rustic, and a firetrap, but it was ours. Many of our immigrant friends were still living in converted barns or chicken coops for years after we were in "our own home." Now that we were all in one place, Dad used his spare hours to continue to make the house more liveable, one bit at a time. We had a backyard outhouse and a pump that drew the freshest, tastiest water just outside the back door. It also had 'drempels' slightly raised wooden thresholds under the doors to keep the drafts out. We learned to lift our feet as we walked around the house, or we'd end up tripping on them.

I have such respect for my parents. They worked so hard, lived so rough, and loved and cared for us so well. I can still see Mom in her worn, apron-covered housedress. Her hair was pulled back and wrapped around a heavy wire to form a neat roll at the nape of her neck. Her knees would be red and calloused from scrubbing the cracked, cheap linoleum floors. She had a kitchen garden in the backyard, which mostly grew beans that were canned to provide our winter vegetables. Hot summer days were busy canning the garden produce, as well as any good deals in seasonal fruits and vegetables. Applesauce or canned red pears were a welcome staple at most meals.

Monday was washday. Whites were boiled on the stove the night before and then carefully washed and wrung out to be hung outside on the clothesline, if possible. Partially dried, frozen pants and towels would come in, stiff and cold, to stand in a corner until they thawed enough to be wrestled to fit over the inside lines. In rainy or winter weather, clotheslines snaked around the ceiling of the main room, where the heat from the one stove also dried the diapers and clothes. Needless to say, we didn't put on clean clothes every day.

My mother always managed to stretch out the paycheque to make sure we were fed. I never remember going hungry. Each week, when the paycheque was brought home, my parents first took out a few precious dollars, which were immediately sealed into the special envelope for church donations. If they didn't do it right away, they knew that there would never be any left over at the end of the week.

I remember shopping once at Kresge's in downtown Hamilton with Mom. They had very beautiful dolls with realistic hair and a beautiful dress. That day, they were on sale. I wanted one so badly. I loved dolls and was always making my own from whatever I could find. Mom didn't have the money, but she did allow me to pick one out, and we put it on layaway for a dollar. When we had the remaining two or three dollars, we could come back and pick it up. She never had those dollars. I probably moved on from that fairly quickly, but it must have been so very hard for my Mom. I appreciated that so much more when I had children of my own.

Our house was probably less than nine hundred square feet in total. Inside the front door you found yourself in a small hallway that led to a living room off to the right, This was used primarily for special occasions. Going through the door straight ahead, you entered another room—we called it the kitchen, and that's what we really lived in. Our house was centred around this one main room, with all the bedrooms and a back kitchen leading to it. This main room housed the stove that both heated the house and cooked the meals, a large dining table, and a day bed under the window for extra seating. This is where we lived; it was the only room in the house that was regularly heated. Here, we shared the simple meals: a pot of boiled potatoes and a fresh seasonal, or a home canned, vegetable on the side; when we had meat, it would have been slowly simmered to produce as much gravy as possible to cover our potatoes for a few meals. We often had carrots, kale, or sauerkraut, cooked with the potatoes in a one-pot meal, which we topped with a sausage. Home-canned applesauce or cooked pears accompanied many meals. Custard pudding, complete with lumps and a gruesome thick skin on the top, would be our dessert, scooped into our scraped-clean dinner plates. Dad would get very upset if we complained about, or wouldn't eat, the food that Mom had prepared. I have learned to eat and appreciate what is served and clean my plate. Except one thing: I won't eat custard puddings.

After the dinner dishes had been cleared away, we would gather around the table to do homework or read the newspaper or a book while Mom put the "little kids" to bed. Then, the coffee percolator would fill the room with its delicious aromas. Right after I was sent to bed, the coffee was poured, the books were put away, and the conversations would begin. I felt so left out.

Grace and I shared a bedroom and a double bed. I had to go into the freezing cold bed, armed with only a hot water bottle, and make it all warm and cozy for when she would finally join me hours later. I remember lying there, tangled in a long flannel nightgown, huddled under the heavy quilts, listening enviously to the murmur of conversation of the family right outside my door.

Often, on a quieter Sunday afternoon, Mom would take out the blue aerogram papers and write lengthy, news-filled letters back home. An aerogram is a very thin, lightweight sheet of paper that was pre-printed to be folded and become its own envelope. This was the cheapest way to send off a letter. Her writing was small and cramped, and every inch, both inside and out, was filled to get as much news as possible. Many of these travelled back and forth across the ocean.

Occasionally, someone would come over with a huge reel-to-reel tape deck, and we children would all speak some message to our faraway relatives. I'm sure my parents added their voices and greetings as well. With long-distance telephone costs, which were charged by the minute, this was a luxury for only the most critical or special occasions. Besides, we didn't have our own telephone for the first number of years. We'd have to run to the neighbours to make or receive a call. Then, we finally got our own. It was a rectangular box on the wall with a crank on one side and a hand piece on the other. Our number was 146Ring13. That meant that one long ring followed by three short ones signalled that the call was for us. We were on a party line (146) and would have to place calls through the operator. It was a leap forward on our way to our personal mobile phones today.

On Sunday evenings, Dad would gather us around him and read us the old classic Dutch children's stories. Or, better yet, he would tell us sentimental stories. He was a good storyteller and would often have difficulty speaking through his own tears.

*Cameras were a luxury in the fifties and the cost to purchase and develop a roll of film just didn't make the list so I'm very thankful that once someone bought a film roll for a Brownie camera for 12 black and white photos and actually saw it through to being developed and printed. A precious gift.*

*Dad in his chair relaxing on a Sunday afternoon. He loved to read.*

*Mom busy cooking dinner. Notice the corner shelf above her head where the family Bible they had received at their wedding was kept safe and handy. This Bible also kept the record of births, baptisms and deaths.*

*Around the table: Diane, Grace, Herman, Johnny (mostly hidden), Harry, Benny, Fenny, Mom, and Blackie the poes.*

*In the living room L to R: Back row: Herman, Benny, Harry, Front: Johnny, Dad, Diane, Grace, Fenny, Mom and baby Margaret.*

*All in a row: Dad, Mom, Grace, Harry, Herman, Benny, Fenny, Johnny and Diane. Baby Margaret was probably already in bed. Diane is wearing the dress I was wearing in the immigration picture.*

*Margaret always wanted a retake that included her. We finally got around to it sixty years later when dining out. From the top: Grace, Harry, Herman, Ben, Fran, John, Diane and Margaret.*

Mom and Dad were strangers in a strange land. Dad became fairly fluent in English because he went out to work, but Mom who served the family and church communities from her home, did not feel very confident speaking English, though she understood it well enough. She was such a humble and unassuming soul. She would, for example, send us to answer the door when strangers knocked, while she kept careful watch from the shadows. However, when there were road crews or construction workers near the house, she wouldn't hesitate to bring them out a hot cup of coffee with some fresh baking to keep them going throughout their day.

The older kids all went to school and learned English pretty quickly. Soon they were speaking English at home too, and we little kids all picked it up. Conversations were mostly bilingual, as my parents continued to speak their heart language. So, I understand Dutch better than I speak it, and even that Dutch is based on the Dutch of the 1940s. Our parents encouraged us to speak English, but I'm a little sad that we didn't also work more at keeping up Dutch. We did learn to read Dutch, and I wrote occasional letters to some cousins back in Holland. Not surprisingly, these cousins were also named Fenny.

This small, unfinished house was our home. It was filled with love and support, and I have many good memories of it.

# CHAPTER 4

## Church: Our Community and Identity

The immigrant church community was so important to our family. Sundays were days of rest. Dad didn't have to go off to work, and he did not even spend time finishing the house on this holy day. Mom would have worked extra hard on Saturday to make sure that the house was clean. We were all bathed, and Sunday outfits were ready for us. She had also made a big pot of soup, baked bread, and probably peeled the potatoes and prepped the vegetables for Sunday dinner. She also allowed herself the luxury to put the unwashed pots and pans under the counter to be scrubbed clean on Monday between doing the loads of laundry. Sundays were to worship the Lord and renew and refresh ourselves so we could meet the pressures and stresses of the new week.

The highlight of Sundays was that we could gather with like-minded people to worship God. We could be with people who understood us—our Dutch language, but also the Dutch culture, the Reformed culture, and the struggles and worries of leaving family and community behind to start over and find your way in a new land. Poverty, being far away from family, all the embarrassing and awkward moments—they could be shared here and maybe laughed about, wept over, or embraced in a comforting, empathetic hug. We would share what we had, whether it was a thermos of coffee, a lead on a job or better housing, a bag of hand-me-downs, or some practical advice.

We would sing the psalms our parents had grown up with, psalms of praise and thanksgiving, as well as laments—the same ones their family were singing back "home." The Bible would be read and preached in our heart language, and its words provided us comfort, direction, and hope. As a child, I did not understand these long and complex sermons, but I learned to sit relatively still and keep myself entertained by making up stories in my head. The peppermints that were doled out during the sermon helped a lot too.

If anything was happening at church, we were there. It started with two services each Sunday in the Labour Temple, with a lunch in between. Holy days were also considered good reasons to gather for a service. Later, there were Bible study societies for men, women, and young people. We were taught the doctrines and history of our faith in Catechism classes and Bible and Church History instruction on Friday evenings (or Saturday morning) for school-aged children. We also enjoyed social events, such as band and choir concerts, Christmas programs, church picnics, missionary visits, etc.

In 2019, I had the privilege of becoming involved with a group of Eritreans as they set up a church in our community. These people—who had had to flee their homelands, spend years in prison, leave family and friends behind to embark on traumatic journeys to come to a place of freedom and opportunity—face some of the same experiences my parents faced. I witnessed and walked with them as they struggled through some of the same kinds of experiences my parents had weathered. Their families and friends are far away, back home, struggling, and they are not able to go back to see them. They are living in shared housing and doing manual labour jobs because their English is not good enough and their qualifications are not accepted here. There are so many regulations and assumptions that they need to become familiar with and learn to navigate. They have arrived in the land of opportunity—the land of new beginnings—but the journey continues to be challenging.

When they get together with their people in a church gathering, they come alive. Their bodies relax, and their faces glow. For those few hours, they know who they are again. These people are their family and their identity. And I remembered my own early years. I can't imagine how we would have managed—especially my parents—without that weekly respite of Sunday Church. It was what connected their present to their past so they could better shape a future. Like my Eritrean friends, there were many Canadians who welcomed, helped, and supported us. Yet, we still need that familiar language, music, and tradition, which speak to our souls and enable us to put down healthy roots in a new soil.

# CHAPTER 5

## Elementary School

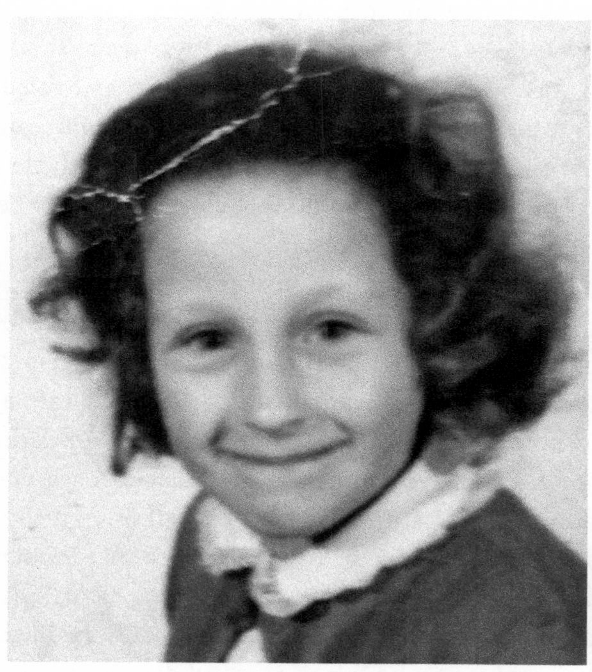

*Me in elementary school.*

When I see how we prepared our children for school and now how much effort goes into getting our grandkids ready for the big adventure of learning, I shake my head in amazement. I do not shake my head at all the effort put into this. No—I shake my head in amazement that I survived my early schooling.

We lived out in the country on a busy highway. The local public school, SS #6 Mount Albion, was about two kilometres from our house, down a gravel side road. It was a small, rural school that had Grades 1 through 8. My brothers all went there, while my oldest sister, Grace, was bussed to Saltfleet Highschool in Stoney Creek.

You had to be six in the calendar year to go to grade one. My birthday was February 24th, so my parents expected to send me the following year, when I would already be six; this would have been a good thing, since I was quite small for my age and very shy. However, the September that I was five, my brothers came home on the first day of school and announced that the principal had said that if anyone had a little brother or sister at home that would be six before the end of February, they could come to grade one.

The next morning, I joined my brothers on the long walk to school, where they escorted me to the first grade classroom and abandoned me there before the teacher or any other students had even arrived. This was my first time stepping into a school, so I had no idea what to expect. Orderly rows of dark, empty wooden desks, shelves with books, a black board across the front, a raised stage at the back—it was all foreign to me. The grade one classroom was the original one-room school that had expanded over the years. Soon, a bell rang, and kids started coming in. I sat myself down at a desk, only to have one of the kids—someone who, on the second day, already knew way more than me about how things worked here—say, "You can't sit there! That's Dougie's desk!" When I moved to another, I was told, "No, not there either; that's Susie's desk!" Thankfully, Mrs. Clark soon appeared and brought me to a desk that I was allowed to sit in, and my schooling began.

My brothers and I walked to school. My kids will tease me when I talk about it. They say, "We know, it was many miles of uphill trudging with dangers lurking behind every bush." It wasn't quite that bad, but to a tiny five-year-old, the two-kilometre walk was long, even though it was relatively flat. Occasionally, if a neighbourhood mother was driving her kids to school, she might think to squeeze me in too. But mostly, we walked.

It wasn't too bad in good weather. Since grade one had a shorter day, I was dismissed an hour before my brothers, so had the choice of walking home alone or waiting for them. When winter came and it was freezing cold, with snowdrifts piled beside the roads and the relentless wind blowing its cold in our faces, it was very long and painful.

When we finally arrived at school and the bell rang, we went to the bathroom to run our frozen hands under the cold-water tap to "warm them up." It was painful! I wore rubber boots with cardboard insoles. Every few days, I would place the boots on a flattened cardboard box, trace them, and cut it out to provide a dry layer of insulation for my feet. Sometimes, I had rubber galoshes to pull on over my shoes. These were okay as long as they didn't have a hole in them. Tape repairs only kept my feet dry for a while. Yes, my fingers and toes were often tingly for quite a while after arriving at my destination, whether it was school or back home.

Our clothing consisted of hand-me-downs and rummage sale finds. We wore a cotton undershirt (hempie), and in the coldest days of winter, we would don a very itchy knitted wool undershirt on top of it. We were allowed to wear a pair of pants under our skirts on the coldest days. Many winter days, I would arrive home so very cold, and Mom would warm my hands in her hands (or armpits) as she welcomed us close to the open oven that was our cooking stove and heat source. Soon, all of us were sitting in a tight circle, with our feet cozied up on the sagging oven door, the smell of wool socks drying, and a hot cup of tea to warm our hands and bellies. It was bliss!

In my first year of school, the class was divided into three reading groups according to ability—that's how primary grades were taught then. I was put into the Cubs, the beginner group. I still remember the day I was called up to read to Mrs. Clark at her desk from one of the *Dick and Jane* readers. I must have adapted to school well enough to be promoted to the second group, the Bombers. I was so proud.

I made it through Mrs. Clark's grade one and went on to Mr. Haddon, the grade two teacher. I was still in the Bombers but was soon promoted to the Jets. I was on a roll. Then, Mr. Haddon asked a group of seven or eight of us to stay after school every day to do some extra work, mainly Arithmetic. He called us the Rockets. This was fine with me, since normally children in second grade were dismissed a half hour before grades three to eight; now I could walk home with my brothers. At the end of the year, all of the Rockets were promoted to grade four. Wow! I got to skip a whole grade! My brother, Benny, was a grade ahead of me; thankfully, he also skipped a grade and went from grade three to grade five.

So, here I was—a very shy, kind of little, seven-year-old beginning grade four. We finally got the luxury of bussing, so now it was just a short walk to the corner, where we met up with other neighbourhood children and entered a warm bus.

I managed to keep up, probably averaging a C+, but it put me at a disadvantage socially. I was not picked on or anything, but I never really felt a part of the social group, usually finding myself alone bouncing my red, white and blue ball against the school wall, skipping, or mostly just watching from the wall. Maybe that's also just me. I still quite enjoy sitting off to the side watching people.

Mr. Haddon taught me for three years—grades two, four, and six. He was a caring and gentle middle-aged man, and I felt safe with him. I can still hear him saying, "The most important question you can ask is 'Why?' Always ask why. Don't just accept things without thinking them through for yourself! It's very important to understand the hows and whys." That teaching alone has made my life far more interesting to this day!

Mr. Coulter taught me in grades four and seven. He was a young teacher, and this was his first assignment out of college. With Brylcreemed hair and clicks on his shoes, he made a dramatic entrance into the little country school. However, some of the students, even back in third and fourth grades were strapping farm boys of fourteen or fifteen years old. In those days, you didn't pass if you didn't meet the standards, so you stayed where you were until you aged out. These boys may not have been able to read and spell, but they weren't going to put up with any nonsense, and soon Mr. Coulter learned to be much more approachable.

My parents never had the opportunity to go past sixth grade, even though both of them would have loved to. My Mom had to quit school at twelve years old to go to work as a servant girl in the home of the schoolmaster, Meester Smit. She lived there, only getting to go home to visit her parents and spend time with her sisters and best friends on a few precious weekends. Occasionally, she would tell stories about how she treasured those weekends at home. She loved and missed her family so much. She was not part of their day-to-day life and missed a lot of watching and helping her younger brothers and sisters grow up. She always wanted to be a teacher but never had the option.

My Dad had to leave school so he could help on the family farm. His younger brother, Albertus, was allowed and encouraged to stay in school, with the hope and expectation that he would study theology and become a 'Dominee." Families had to make their choices. Unfortunately, this younger brother died when he was eighteen. He was studying when a severe thunderstorm sprang up. His mother urged him to come and sit in the main room with them to stay safe. As he walked by the window, a lightning bolt struck him, and he died instantly. This tragedy, understandably, left deep scars on the family.

So, given their short schooling experience and unfamiliarity with the English language and curriculum, helping me with school was not something my parents felt comfortable with. Big brothers could help a bit, but mostly it was, "You'll have to figure it out the best you can. So sorry, I don't know how to help you." That must have been so difficult for my parents, and for Mom, especially; it was a constant reminder of what she couldn't do. She always encouraged me to stay in school and lived along with me in my dream to become a teacher.

I was off to a good start. In addition to the reading, writing, and arithmetic I had decided on my career. I had learned perseverance, self-reliance, and a love of learning and discovering. Mr. Haddon's reminder to ask the "whys" has helped keep my life interesting and on track.

# CHAPTER 6

## Faith: It's Simple

God and faith were the core of our lives. Yes, church was a big part of it. But our daily lives revolved around, and were anchored by, an absolute but simple trust that we were loved and cared for by a good and loving Father in Heaven.

Each meal was officially sanctioned by expressing our thankfulness that our needs were provided for once again, and asking for a blessing on the food as well as the works of our hands and hearts. Our growly stomachs had to be content with the smells until the formal prayer was complete and we had, in turn from oldest to youngest, added our own rote prayer: "*Here zegen deze spijze. Amen*" (Lord, bless this food, Amen.).

After sharing the simple, lovingly prepared food over small talk and laughter, and probably some tantrums and bickering, the old family Bible that my parents had received at their marriage was taken down from its honorary perch, and Dad read a chapter. He would begin at Genesis, and one chapter per day, we would eventually arrive at Revelation. Then, he would begin at the beginning again. After the Bible reading, and maybe a question or two to keep us on our toes, we joined in prayer. This time, with bellies satisfied, we brought the needs of the family, church, community, and world before God, in full expectation that God would hear, care, and answer. Once again, you couldn't be caught with your mind wandering, for when Dad pronounced the "Amen," the children, again from oldest to youngest, repeated "*Here, dank U voor deze spijze, Amen*" (Lord, thank you for this food, Amen). Woe to the child who wasn't paying sufficient attention and got the two prayers mixed up!

Mom would sometimes read us Bible stories from a well-worn Dutch Children's Story Bible. There were few pictures, only occasional line drawings on the side margins. I can remember a simple sketch of a very friendly-looking older man lying on a cloud, peering through a break, gazing lovingly at the Earth along a sunbeam. I can still see it in my mind's eye, and I'm sure the kindness and the caring of that image has shaped and influenced my "picture" of who God is. Still today, sunbeams make me feel safe and closer to God.

This memory is surprising to me because we were taught that you cannot, and must not, draw a picture of God in any way; no picture or image can ever capture who God is. "You shall not make an idol" is a very serious Biblical command that came with long-lasting consequences. Yet, we do need to be able to identify with God in some way. This simple line drawing probably added to my perception that God was elderly, male, and separate from us, above the clouds somewhere. It's still an image of God that influences not only my thinking, but that also reflects the common perception of our culture. It's extremely limited as a Biblical portrayal, but as a young child, it was enough.

My childhood understanding of God was also very much shaped by the love, security, and care I received from my parents. They were my first tangible picture and experience of God's love and character, even though they would have been the first to declare that they were a very small and imperfect image. They loved me, provided for me, protected me, inspired me, and taught me how to live. They instilled rhythms of worship, a love and need of community, personal responsibility, and a vision to pursue dreams and take risks. They walked by faith every day and in every way. It was the only thing that kept them going.

Mom was quieter about her faith, but she lived it so well. To me and my siblings, she was a gentle, loving spirit that would rock us on her lap or shelter us behind her ever-present wrap-around apron. She would feel and soothe our cold, fear, or sickness. She often needed to implore us to stop our bickering and just get along. "*Alle gekheid op en stokje; stokje in de sloot!*" she would say in exasperation. It is an old Dutch expression meaning, "Put all the silliness on a stick, and throw the stick in the ditch." She was a peacemaker.

Her sweet, clear voice was often singing the old psalms, hymns, and folk songs while she uncomplainingly did her endless chores. Our home was nothing fancy, but she did her best to make it welcoming and cozy. Cheerful geraniums graced the windowsills, and a thick Dutch table rug added sophistication to the worn wooden table after dinner as we all pulled our chairs in close. Mom's hands were seldom idle, and her heart was always ready to bless someone with a warm smile or an empathetic ear. Our family was blessed, but so were the many others who often joined our circle for an hour or two of feeling loved and included.

Dad was always ready to talk about his faith, at home, at church or anywhere people were ready for conversation. He lived it as well in so many ways. He worked long days and then evenings were often devoted to 'church work'.

My faith as a child was a simple trust: God is in heaven, my parents are here, all's okay with the world. Besides the family prayer times and conversations, I had my own practice of desperate prayers. These included, "Dear God, please don't let the teacher see that I didn't finish my homework!!" and "Dear God, please, please, please don't let me fail this test even though I didn't study for it and deserve to fail!!!" and "Dear God, I'm so cold and it's still such a long walk before I'm home!" And the God of grace, second chances, and third and fourth chances… always heard me. I was sure of that. And I usually also said, "Thank You!!"

# CHAPTER 7

## My Siblings

My siblings are the people that understand me better than anyone else. For the first years of our lives, the years when so much of our character is shaped, these are the people who are there every day. We come from the "same stock," and we have many shared memories.

*Grace at school in Holland*

Grace is nine years older than me, but to me, she ranked up there right beside Mom and Dad. By the time I actually have memories of her, she was a teenager, and a very responsible one at that. When I look at pictures of her when she was fifteen or so, she looks like one of the adults.

She had also had a head start in school back in Holland. She went to kindergarten, but then just missed the cut-off date for grade one. Instead of having her do kindergarten again, my parents kept her home and hired a tutor. Back in Holland, they had money for things like that. When she was finally allowed to go to first grade, she was quickly advanced to third.

When we arrived in Canada, she was initially placed in her age category, but when she had mastered enough English, she was advanced again. Grace graduated from grade ten just after her fifteenth birthday and began working the lunch counter at Kresge's in downtown Hamilton. She then found a position in the Bank of Montreal, where she rapidly advanced to teller, and then to head teller.

When Grace got her driver's licence at sixteen, Dad sold the old Plymouth he was driving and bought two tiny Hillmans—a grey one and a blue one, so they could each drive into the city to work. We used both vehicles to transport the family to church on Sundays. It was a win-win situation.

*Highschool years*

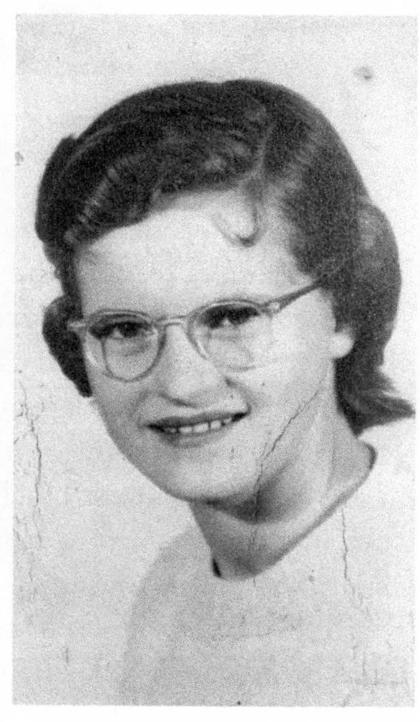

*A very competent oldest child, sister and banker.*

*Harry*

My oldest brother, Harry, was seven years older than me. He spent hours reading and was happy to share what he was learning. He particularly loved learning and using big words, like "sesquipedalian." Harry is quieter and more introspective, and he has always been a gentle, loving, and supportive person. He had some pet bunnies for a while. He would let them loose in the daytime to feast on the delicious clover and put safely back in their cage before sunset. He also had homing pigeons, which he kept in our attic. Harry was also the maker. There wasn't money for games or toys, but Harry would design and build board games to keep us entertained.

*Herman*

Herman, the next in the line and five years my senior, was the steady, caring, and dependable one. He was the one that I remember walking to and from school with, knowing he was looking out for me. The others were great too, but in my memories, it's Herman who was always there to support and protect. He didn't enjoy school very much but happily went off each afternoon to the dairy farm across the street to help farmer Bill with the chores. I would sometimes go along and be allowed to help put the milking machines together and fill the grain bin.

One day, walking home from the farm along the highway, a passing car lost its front hood; it flew off and hit Herman right in the face. He was knocked unconscious and bleeding. While Mom and Dad and the older brothers ran out, they ordered the rest of us to stay put. We could only watch and worry through the front window. It was terrifying watching this through the glass. At first, I was sure that he was dead. I was busy making flowers out of paper, and I determined to decorate his grave with them. Thankfully, that wasn't necessary. After an ambulance ride and a week or so in hospital, he came home ready to regain his strength. He did make the newspaper, though, and he was a bit of a celebrity at school. Despite his newfound fame, he wasn't destined to remain in school. Herman quit school after Grade 8 and went to work full time.

*Ben*

Benny, as we called him back then, was far more outgoing and confident than me. He was, and is, seldom at a loss for words and was able to engage in conversation with almost anyone. I so envied him for that. Our birth years are three calendar years apart, though he's just two years and three months older. Early schooling put us just one grade apart. Ben is the one I played and fought with the most. I think we were good for each other in our differences. Ben often led the way and explored new avenues that opened new possibilities for me. I learned to follow him, but also to, then, chart my own course.

*Harry, Johnny, Benny and Herman*

*Johnny*

Little Johnny was two years and three months younger than me, yet he seemed so much younger than that. He was four grades behind me in school. He loved being outdoors and playing hard. He was ever curious, unable to sit still for long, and very sweet. He played mostly with his two younger sisters. We called these three "the little kids."

Once, when Dad made a run to a neighbourhood grocery store, Ben, Johnny, and I were allowed to go along. Johnny and I shared the backseat while Ben chatted with Dad up front. Suddenly, Johnny stood up to join the conversation (long before seatbelts and safer door handles were a thing), grabbing the door handle; the door opened, and Johnny tumbled out onto the road! I was so shocked that I couldn't even speak to tell Dad what had happened. It wasn't until Ben turned around—thankfully only seconds later—that he raised the alarm. Johnny was lying on the shoulder of the road, and the car behind us managed to stop before hitting him. Dad and Johnny made the ambulance trip to the hospital as kind strangers drove Benny and me home and let Mom know what had happened. Thankfully, he was not seriously injured, and he returned home after a few days. He still has the scars on his forehead.

*Johnny and me. I was probably in grade one.*
*I remember wearing my hair in a curl on top of my head.*

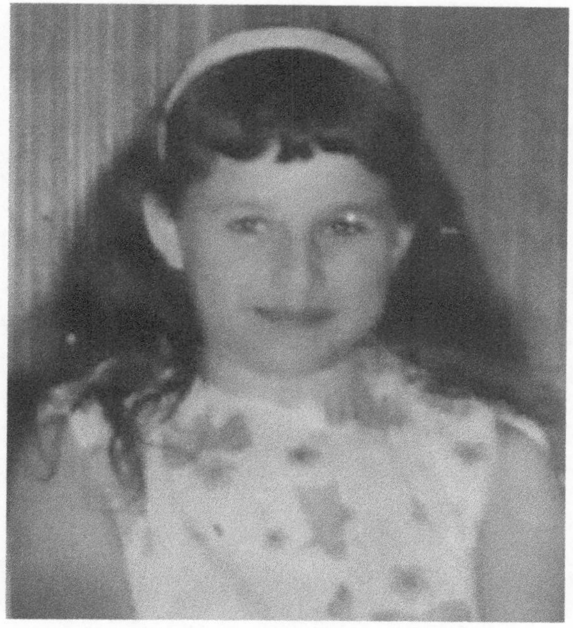

*Diane*

Diane was born just after my fifth birthday. Baby Diane was a beautiful charmer who would quietly observe the world from the corner of her eyes. The six older siblings all had a namesake to identify with—both sets of grandparents, an uncle who died at a tragically young eighteen years of age, and my Dad. Diane was given three Dutch names, but we always called her Diane. Imagine, three names! Some of us had one. Some of us had two. But she received three: Dina, Hendrika, Johanna. Dad had elderly relatives who had remained childless and had no one to carry their names into the future. So, Diane received that responsibility. I loved the poetry of her name. And, being one that had only one name, maybe I also envied the extravagance of three!

*Margaret*

Margaret was born the September I entered second grade. I remember coming home from school that September day and being surprised to find that Mom wasn't there. Instead, a girl that we knew through church was there to welcome us home with the news that we had a new sister. This was the first I had ever heard of it. Mom's aprons had done a good job of keeping it hidden, and pregnancy just wasn't something you talked about, especially with kids. I probably wasn't the most observant child either. I do remember visiting Mom and the baby in a small clinic operated by a Dutch doctor. When they both came home a week or so later, I concluded that Mom must have been sick and had to go to the hospital. When she was well enough to come home again, they gave her a baby to take along as a gift. So much for my sex education! Blond curls, spunky, and cute, Margaret was a welcome addition to complete our family.

Either Diane or Margaret could have been named in honour of Mom, with a name similar to Siena but more Canadian, like Sylvia. But, instead, this tiny bundle was named after the neighbour, Margaret Robinson.

Margaret Robinson, and her husband, Ken, and their son, Kenny (Johnny's age), lived next door. Well, there was a field between our houses, but there was also a well-worn pathway through the middle of it, going from our back door straight to theirs. Margaret and Ken must have been a lifeline for Mom. Dad put in long days at work, the older kids were in school, and she was in that tiny little house with whatever number of babies and toddlers they had at the time. Margaret's friendship and helpfulness meant the world to her. Both Johnny and I played with Kenny. We taught him some Dutch, confusing his mom when he would ask for a *boterham* (sandwich). I adopted his doll and raised it as my own.

Diane and Margaret, were treated like twins. They were Mom's little treasures. She finally had a bit of extra time and energy to enjoy her babies and toddlers. Where one went, the other went. What one got, the other got. There still weren't many material goods to spoil them with, but they weren't pushed out of lap space, or even crib space, by new babies. I'm so glad that Mom got that gift of being able to take some time to just enjoy her babies. However, I did think they were spoiled rotten, and I felt like Cinderella who had to do all the work, with little appreciation too, while the cute little princesses got to play.

*Diane and Margaret, such little cuties.*

One year, on Christmas Eve, the two little girls were both dancing with excitement while Mom was filling the galvanized aluminum tub that was our bath. The next day would see us going to church in the morning for a fairly regular service. But then, in the afternoon, we would go back and have a party. Christmas carols, a sentimental Christmas story, and all the children would receive a book, an orange, and some candy. Dad sometimes told the story, but this year, our big sister Grace was going to do it.

To save a bit of time, Mom put the hot water she had heated on the stove into the tub first, and then she hastened to refill the huge pot with cold water to cool it down. The girls sat on the edge of the tub, tipping it over and spilling the very hot water over them. I managed to grab Margaret out, so she and I had only a few burnt spots on our feet.

But Diane was in bad shape. She had fallen back into the tub and sustained significant burns. Mom stripped her, wrapped her in a sheet, and ran off to the neighbours, who drove them to the doctor's office. From there, she was taken to the hospital, where she had to stay for about a month. My parents got to see her during the one-hour visitors' slot on the weekends. These were hard times for Diane and all of us.

That Christmas turned out differently than we expected. I had to wear Mom's slipper on my burnt foot to the celebration. My book was *Mary Jones and Her Bible.*

*Mom with the three 'Canadezen", Johnny, Diane and Margaret.*

*Mom, Dad, Johnny, Diane and Margaret at Niagara Falls.*

These are the people that made up my world—my second ring of security. We share experiences and memories, and we soon learned to look out for one another.

# CHAPTER 8

## Extended Family

My parents and siblings were the inner circle of my world back then, but extended family formed a very important next ring. Since most of them were far away in Holland, the ones we had close by were extra special.

*Uncle Gerry, Mom's younger but oldest brother.*

I have already mentioned Oom Gerrit (Uncle Gerry Hutten) and Tante Janke (Aunt Yanka). They were the ones who had arrived in Canada the year before we did and took us into their home until Dad had our house built enough for us to move in. When we arrived, they had no children. They had buried their only son, Harry, back in Holland after he died of cancer at the age of four. This was such an unimaginably difficult thing for them.

Thankfully, and joyfully, after becoming a bit settled in Canada, they received more children, the cousins I grew up with. Grace, the eldest, is a few years younger than me, and we spent many hours playing together as kids. Later, their family was enriched with John, Linda (with the second name Fenny), Jerry, Theresa, and Tim.

*The joy and love on Uncle Gerry's face as he holds his precious gift Grace.*

*Uncle Gerry, Tante Janke with Grace and John.*

We visited them every few weeks, usually on a Saturday afternoon. They didn't live very close to us and belonged to a different congregation, so those Saturday visits are what I remember most. After a number of years in Aldershot, they moved to Lowbanks, just outside of Dunnville, which was about an hour's drive away from us. Uncle Gerry got a job managing a farm there. They first lived in a section of the barn that had been converted to make it liveable, and later, the farmer moved an actual house onto the property for them.

My brothers, Herman and Harry, spent a few summers there helping Uncle Gerry on the farm when they were young teens.

We would go out on Saturdays to visit them all, and sometimes we got to ride Nellie, the old horse down the lane. Going out was calm and safe, but when her head was turned back in the direction of the barn, the tired old horse would suddenly take off, making for a far more interesting ride.

In the afternoons, we would often end up at Long Beach, Lake Erie, to play in the waves and the sand. The adults would form a protective circle with towels so we could change on the beach. Tante Janke was a great cook, and she was very resourceful at stretching the pennies that were few and far between, so she knew how to make these days so memorable. She was also a very good seamstress. I have memories of her coming for the day to mend, alter, and maybe even sew us some new clothes.

*Uncle John Hutten*

Uncle John Hutten, Mom's little brother, also got the immigration itch, and when he was nineteen, he moved to Canada. He stayed with his brother, my Uncle Gerry, who was still living in Aldershot at the time. Uncle John was the fun uncle. He would suddenly appear, maybe on his motorcycle, to take us all for a little ride or for a party—it always seemed like a party when he was around.

Uncle John and Aunt Jane's wedding was very memorable. They got married Friday evening in a ceremony presided over by the United Church minister, since our ministers were not yet licensed to perform weddings. Then we partied! There were songs, skits, and even some folk dances! At the time, weddings were a great excuse to unleash our creativity. People you saw sitting soberly in the church pews on Sundays, or having serious discussions over a cup of well-percolated coffee and a slice of *koek*, now got up on stage and performed hilarious skits. These skits were even better when they poked fun at the bride or groom. Poems and ABCs highlighting the bride's and groom's life stories were tucked in between enthusiastically sung songs from a song sheet filled with hymns, patriotic songs, and some fun songs. Then, we would all jump up from our seats to join a circle dance with music blaring. We had so much fun!

At the end of the evening, Uncle John's bride, my Aunt Jane, went home again with her parents, and Uncle John returned to his place. Sunday morning, the bride put on her wedding dress again, and we all dressed in our new dresses and formal suits as we waited downstairs for the regular Sunday worship service to begin. Then, we all paraded down the aisle, and they repeated their vows once more before God and the church. After that, they finally got to go home together.

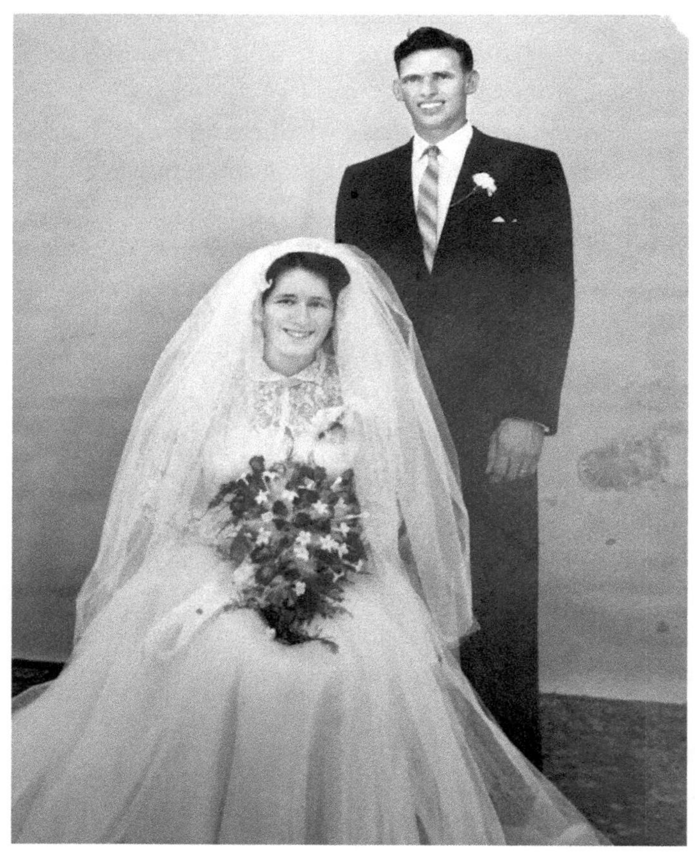

*Aunt Jane and Uncle John*

*Uncle John and Aunt Jane's children LtoR Back Jeannette, Frances; centre: Harry, Gary and David; front: Nancy and John. Not yet born: Scott*

*Gerry and Jannie with Mom and Dad.*

Gerry Jans is my cousin, but in my heart he's my big brother. He is the eldest son of my Dad's sister, and his special connections with our family go way back to the beginning of the Second World War. Back in the 1930s, Dad's sister, Tante Zwaantje, had married Oom Hendrieks, a German, and joined him on his farm in Germany. This farm backed right on to the German–Dutch border, not too far from where my Dad and Mom lived in Holland, on the old family farm. Dad's Mom, my Oma, had died, so when my parents got married, they moved in with Opa to run the household and care for him.

When war broke out, Gerry was sent to live on the family farm with his Opa and my parents during the school year, so he could continue in the Christian school in Holland. At school breaks, under the watchful eyes of my Dad and his own, he would sneak back and forth across the border to spend some time with his family. My uncle, a German citizen, was a very gentle soul and a strong Christian. He used his strategic location on the border to help commandeered Dutch citizens sneak back home after they'd escaped the Germans. He would hide them by day, and when the soldiers guarding the border were not looking, he would escort them across from the back of his farm.

Gerry lived with my family during the war years, from 1940 to 1945. After the war, Gerry's parents left Germany and moved to Holland to care for my Opa, and my parents moved into their own place. So, Gerry could live with his own parents and brothers again without really having to move. Of course, I only know of this through stories, since it preceded my birth by quite a bit.

Once we were all living in Canada, Gerry's parents also decided to emigrate. However, their application was denied. Gerry, being an adult by then, applied on his own and was approved. So, he packed his bags and moved to our area in 1953. Since our tiny house was already bursting at the seams, he found a boarding house and contented himself with visiting frequently.

I loved Gerry. As soon as he would walk in, I'd be all over him. My place was on his lap. Then, one day, he came with a girl named Jannie. She sat with her smiley face right next to him, and they both looked so happy. I was not happy! So, I crawled onto his lap, looked her in the eye, and made myself clear: "This is *my* Gerry!" She got the message.

She married him and has been an excellent partner for many years, but she still remembers and recognizes my four-year-old claim. And she won my heart, too. When Gerry and Jannie would drop by for a summer evening visit, they would sometimes bring a pint block of Neapolitan ice cream. A pint of ice cream isn't much bigger than a pound of butter, but my talented Mom was able to get out the big knife, heat it slightly, and slice the pint so we all got a delicious treat.

Gerry and Jannie's wedding was also a highlight for me, and it was one of the few times I got a new dress that was purchased just for me. It was a very pretty baby blue dress with a white lace trim down the front. I felt so beautiful!

*Jannie and Gerry*

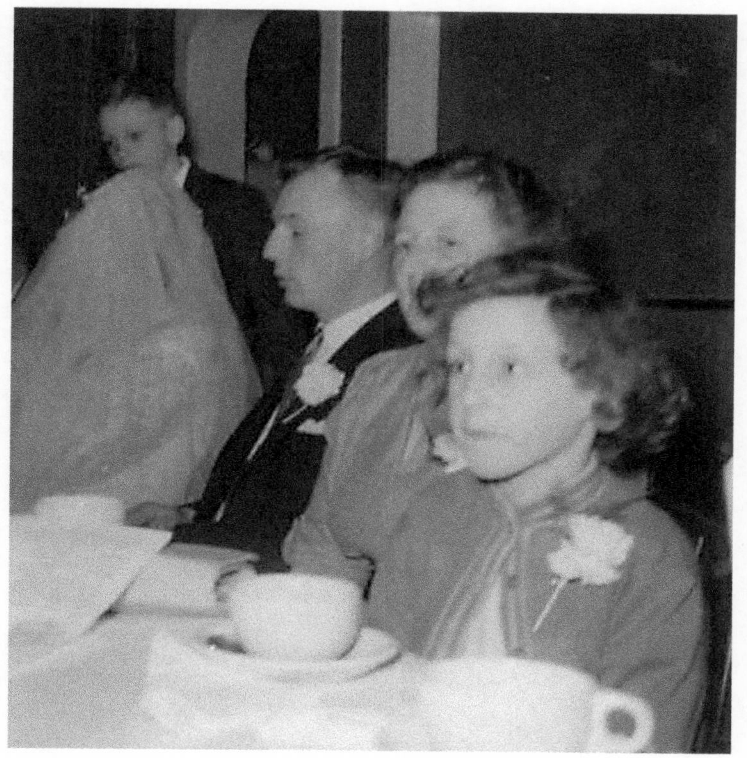

*Me with my new dress and even a corsage, Mom, Gerry and Jannie*

These were the family members that I had on this side of the ocean. They shared our common roots and our immigrant struggles. They were there for birthdays, weddings, births, and any significant milestones. We were also there to help each other get over a hurdle, or just spend a fun day or evening together to relax, build memories, and enjoy life's goodness. They are still here. Uncle Gerry, Tante Janke, and just recently, Uncle John, have passed on, but Aunt Jane, Gerry, Jannie, and the cousins are still part of our lives.

# CHAPTER 9

## Opa and Opoe Come for a Visit (1958)

With three children in Canada, my grandparents were eager to see how we were all doing and what life in Canada was really like. They had grandchildren they had never seen, other than in the few pictures that travelled across the ocean in carefully sealed envelopes. Opa was a tall, calm, confident looking man. Opoe was a tiny woman with sparkly eyes and a fun-loving character. They were humble and unassuming people with a very real and simple faith. They dressed in the old traditional fashion for the common people—for Opa, a black suit, cap, and wooden shoes, and for Opoe, black, ankle-length, long-sleeved dresses and the traditional white lace cap with a fancy ruffle along the bottom for Sundays. (I have the last of Opoe's white lace hats framed and hanging in my bedroom)

In 1958, they were making the trip of a lifetime. They had seldom ventured very far from their tiny village, going only where feet and bicycle could take them. They boarded the train in sleepy little Gramsbergen for the trip to the big city of Rotterdam.

Their oldest daughter, Mom's sister, Tante Zwaantje, joined them on the train for a few stops. Since her husband was a conductor, she got to travel for free. Everyone they met on the journey had to hear the story of them going to Canada to visit three of their children. Such excitement needed to be shared!

They sailed on a passenger ship from Rotterdam to New York. On the way, they experienced a huge storm. All the passengers were panicking, and they were sure they were going to drown when Opa stood up by the railing and, in his loud but calm voice, assured them that they would be okay. He then led them in prayer. The storm stopped, and they all arrived safely in New York.

Uncle John picked them up from the harbour, and they spent one month with each of their kids. I had no idea what it was like to have grandparents until then, other than through stories and letters. Now, it was real! They were real. Their love was real. In those precious weeks, we made great memories.

I remember walking along the road with Opa in his *klompen* (wooden clogs), hands clasped behind his back. He would talk with anyone we came across, even if there was a language barrier. And I can still picture Opoe, braiding her tiny neat little braid every morning and twisting it into a tiny bun at the nape of her neck. Opoe had always had dirt floors in her house. They were swept clean, and every Saturday they would spread fresh clean sand in intricate patterns. But they were dirt floors. One morning, when Opoe wanted some fresh tea, she quickly dumped the old, cold tea under the table, only to realize that our cheap linoleum wouldn't absorb the liquid. With a bit of an embarrassed twinkle, she laughed about it and promised to clean it up later.

Opoe always wore black. But her new Sunday dress actually had the tiniest white dots in the pattern, and she worried that this might be too fancy for church. She also had a black-brimmed hat that had a white silk rose adorning it, but she had to remove the rose. It just was too impractical.

Of course, they came to church with us. In Holland, they had stayed with the original church and had not "become liberated," but that didn't seem to put a damper on things here. They accompanied us to church every Sunday. Every week during this time, we had a Dutch service in the morning and an English service in the afternoon. They came along to both and joined in the singing of the English songs by singing the Dutch words, which they knew by heart. The melodies were all the same.

It was so great to have them. I remember that my front teeth were fairly new, and they were growing in a bit crooked, so Opoe showed me how to straighten them by putting pressure on them with my fingers to push them straight. There wasn't money for dentists, except when terrible toothaches required that we pull a decayed tooth, so having straighter teeth was a do-it-yourself project. I'm sure it helped a bit, but that tooth eventually chipped when brother Herman hit me on the back of the head while I was licking my plate. So, while it may have been straighter, it was also the fraction of a tooth!

I don't remember a lot of specifics about their visit, but it felt like a rich time where we all felt particularly loved and special. For my Mom and Dad, it must have been such a special time. Mom seemed to laugh much more when her family was around. We had family get-togethers, too. By then, Uncle John was married, and their son Harry was a babe in arms. The last family get-together was on Labour Day, out at Uncle Gerry and Tante Janke's farm in Lowbanks.

We had enjoyed three glorious months of getting to know them, and then September came, and Uncle John drove them back to New York. As he was walking them up the gangplank of their ship for the return voyage, he heard a voice from the railing say, "Oh good, the old man is here again. Now I know we'll make it safely!"

It would be eleven years before I would see them again, when I travelled to Holland and saw them in their own home. As a child, you live much more in the moment and in your own bubble. Also, the language was a barrier, since I already did not feel comfortable enough in Dutch to hold lengthy conversations with them. However, they were certainly more real to me, and I longed to get to know them better. That was why a trip to Holland was my first priority as an adult with my own money.

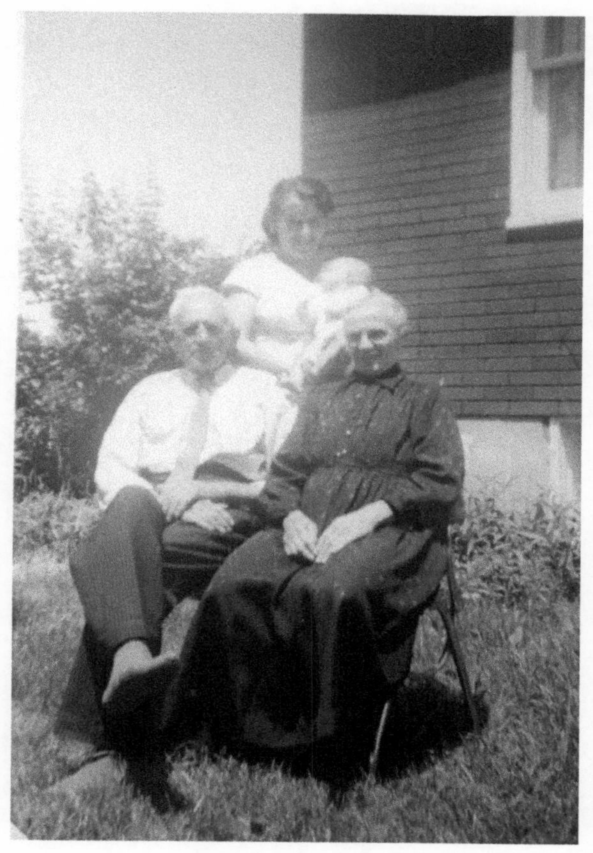

*Opa and Opoe with Aunt Jane and Harry.*

*Opa pretending he can drive Uncle John's truck.*

*Opoe and Opa with their three Canadian children.*

*Opoe and Opa and their Canadian family.*

# THE SECOND DECADE

# CHAPTER 10

## Aldershot Again

The summer I was eleven, we moved. We sold that little "handyman special." Over the years, we had added an indoor kitchen sink complete with (cold) running water, an indoor toilet, a beautiful "antique" claw foot bathtub in the open basement beside the sump pump, and a gas furnace.

Aldershot once again became home, this time on Unsworth Road instead of Gallagher Road. Though this house was old—it was one of three houses that had been built as part of the original Unsworth Farm—it was a definite step up for us. It was probably twice the size of our old home, with three fairly large bedrooms upstairs. Now all four of us girls shared the big room, with two double beds taking up most of the space. The four boys slept on two sets of bunk beds in a smaller room across the hall. And Mom and Dad got their own bedroom at last, though it was the smallest one.

We now had indoor plumbing with hot and cold running water in the kitchen and a three-piece bathroom. It was heated by two gas-stove heaters, one in the dining room and one in the front room. The stovepipe from the dining room ran up through one of the bedrooms, mine, thankfully. It provided a bit of extra warmth. In the morning, we would grab our clothes and run down to dress by the warm stove. In winter, the front room would be closed off, except for special occasions, to conserve energy.

In return, my Dad and brothers had to work in Unsworth's Greenhouses. In the summers this was extremely hot, uncomfortable work, and the days were long. However, it was a good step for the family. With Dad and Herman working full time in the greenhouses and Harry working summers while completing high school, life was a bit better. Grace was doing well in the bank and saving to get married. Diane and Margaret were now both in school, so Mom got some part-time work cleaning houses for neighbours. We were now living in a well-to-do suburban neighbourhood. While this was extra busyness for an already hard-working Mom, she really enjoyed being able to get out of the house and make some connections with neighbours. They, of course, loved her, and the few extra dollars she contributed to our family income gave her a new sense of self-worth.

*909 Unsworth Rd. LtoR back: Fran, Ben, Mom, Dad, Grace, Herman, Harry; front: Margaret, Diane, Johnny*

When we moved, my Mom suggested that I change my name. I had always been called Fenny. "Now," she said, "why don't you call yourself Frances?" I like that my Mom gave me both my Dutch and my Canadian name, and I still proudly use them—Fennigje on official documents and Fran for the rest.

We spent two years on Unsworth Road. I went to Fairfield Elementary, a two-storey brick heritage-type building, for Grade eight. Johnny was in fourth grade, and Diane and Margaret both started school here, Diane beginning first grade and Margaret in kindergarten. I have good memories of this school. I felt welcomed and included and soon made friends. It had amenities not yet offered in the rural Mount Albion School, such as a gymnasium, a music program, and more specialized teachers for various subjects. We walked a few short blocks to school along quiet streets, and then we went home again for lunch. This time, it was usually in the company of classmates who were friendly and fun company.

I became very good friends with Elaine Scott, a girl who lived down the street. The two of us spent hours together at her house, mine, or halfway between, sitting on our bikes chatting up a storm until the streetlights came on. Elaine only had one sister who was considerably older than she was. Her parents also really liked to golf, so they would often leave her to fend for herself after school, including dinner, so Elaine was always happy if I came to keep her company. She also loved being in our busy, noisy home. Elaine and I remained good friends long after we moved away; she even came to live with our family when she was going through some struggles in her late teens. Sadly, we lost touch after she got married and moved farther away.

Aldershot High was a bit of a longer walk, and it was a new experience. It was a brand-new, welcoming school. We had lunch in a cafeteria every day. Though I packed my own sandwich and snack, there was usually a bit of money to buy an ice cream treat for dessert. Here's where I caught up with Ben while he repeated Grade 9. He was just too busy being social and enjoying the extracurricular opportunities (especially drama) to pay enough attention to his studies.

Hannon had been rural, composed mostly of farms and old families with very modest economic situations. Aldershot was definitely middle- to upper-middle-class suburban living. Along the lakefront, very expensive homes took advantage of the beautiful views. Next to that were comfortable homes on large landscaped lots. People were friendly and welcoming. Besides making the transition from childhood to my teen years, Aldershot helped me transition to a more sophisticated suburban culture.

# CHAPTER 11

## Burlington (1963)

Two years later, just as I was entering tenth grade, we moved into central Burlington. Dad had found a better job at Consumer's Lumber in Hamilton, so we had to move out of the Unsworth Road house that had come with his old job. But, with more family members working and contributing, Dad and Mom had been able to save enough to put a down payment on our own home again. Harry had finished high school and was working in an upscale furniture store in Hamilton, and Herman had found a good job in Burlington.

This home on Graham's Lane was in a unique area of the city. Downtown was in walking distance, but from the main street, we had a short walk through an industrial area, across a little-used railroad track, and find ourselves on a private road. There were about half a dozen houses, a few small businesses, and a market gardening farm on our road.

*1335 Graham's Lane, Burlington, Ontario*

Now, home was a large old house on an acre with two beautiful ancient chestnut trees gracing the front lawn. This was the original house for a larger farm that had since been subdivided. It had four bedrooms upstairs, as well as a huge glassed-in sunporch running along the whole back of the house. This became my bedroom for a while, and I loved the thrill of climbing between icy sheets in the winter and being able to see the stars or be part of whatever the weather brought. This was my first time having a bedroom to myself, as Grace got married a few months after we moved in. Downstairs was a huge living room, a formal dining room, and a sizeable kitchen. A mudroom for laundry was our back entrance. Off the living room was a smaller sunroom that became an office space.

Dad was working at Consumer's Lumber until he had an accident where he lost a thumb and finger to a saw. Then, through a church acquaintance, he found work as a caretaker for Mary Hopkins Elementary School in Waterdown. While the work was not too exciting, he did love being in a school, where he could chat with the teachers and watch the kids. He worked his way from the afternoon shift cleaning classrooms to being the head caretaker. Sunday afternoons Dad and Mom, usually with Diane and Margaret in the back seat, would drive to the school to make sure the furnace was working, and the classrooms would be warm and inviting for Monday morning.

He was also very involved in church leadership, often serving as an elder, and sometimes even chairman of the Church Council. As kids, we also knew that we had a responsibility as the children of one of the elders. This was more implicit than explicit. I remember one occasion when I wanted to go to see a movie. *Dr. Zhivago* was the big hit in the theatres, and sixteen-year-old me and many of my friends were also interested in seeing it. But going to the movie theatre was considered risky—it was a place where the devil enticed you to go astray. A few of my friends and I planned to go. We all asked our parents beforehand and got permission. One of them was the pastor's son, and another's father was an elder. The following day, I was enthusiastically telling my friend all about it. She was shocked and asked if my parents knew that I had gone. "Oh yes," I said. "I asked Dad, and he said I could go." So, she went home and asked her Dad, saying that Fran and these other friends had been given permission to go. That evening, my Dad got an angry telephone call from her Dad. I was sitting nearby, eavesdropping. He listened respectfully and then responded, "It's my business what my children do, and I will make that based on what I think is the best. It's none of your business!" After he got off the phone, he admitted that he had not realized that *Dr. Zhivago* was a movie, but he supported and trusted me.

*Dad 1978*

Mom was a good support for Dad in his church leadership, and she also used her gifts in the church community. She was a good listener and a warm and inviting friend to many. I remember coming home sometimes to find another lady from the church pouring her heart out to my Mom. Or another woman with deep anxiety issues, afraid to be alone, would spend many evenings at our house while her husband was busy with church work. Mom had that calm, accepting character that invited people to trust her. She was well loved and respected, but she was unassuming and felt very awkward in the spotlight. Actually, both of my parents were trusted and respected. Many of our friends would love to come to our place just so they could talk with my parents.

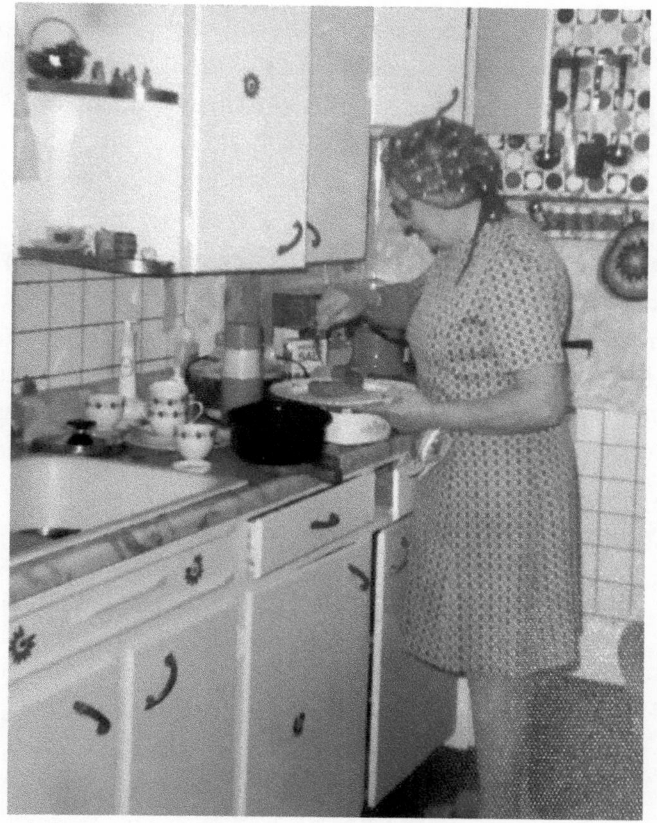

*Mom spent so many hours in the kitchen. Saturdays she washed her hair and I put the rollers in, one more step in the preparations for Sunday.*

My parents celebrated their twenty-fifth wedding anniversary on July 12, 1965. They had seen and experienced so much, including getting a foothold in a new land. We eight children were now almost all double digits, and Sidney, the first grandchild, had enriched all of our lives. We bought them a brand-new teak queen sized bedroom set. It was the first new bedroom furniture for them, at least since we'd immigrated.

My aunt and uncle from Brazil came up to help celebrate. We had a big silver anniversary party in the church basement, complete with the expected and anticipated skits, songs, and poems. Then we sent them off on a holiday.

They'd never, ever, gone off on a holiday before. Monday morning, they packed their suitcase and set off for beautiful cottage country, Bracebridge. They enjoyed the drive up there, went out for dinner, and found a place to stay. The next morning, they looked at each other and said, "Now what do we do?" Neither one knew. So, they got back in the car and drove home. We had been expecting a fun week by ourselves, but we were both happy and sad to see them back on Tuesday afternoon. They knew work and serving others. They didn't know how to relax and just enjoy themselves.

*Me, Diane and Margaret on the couch.*

These were my teen years. I transferred to Burlington Central High School, the original, well-established school right in the downtown core. Central was a large school with about eighteen hundred students, much larger than I was used to. Here's where I muddled my way through trying to understand and interpret poetry and bluff my way through assignments and discussions on classics I couldn't bring myself to actually fully read. I learned about mostly English and American history, French, a year of German, and as much Maths and Sciences as was required to graduate and be eligible for university. I also took Home Economics all the way through, using my sewing skills to add to my wardrobe during those high school years. My standards have since been raised, so I no longer sew for myself or anyone I love.

I have good memories of some of the teachers who tried their best to open my mind to information or inspire me to think, feel, and participate. Mr. Kalbfleisch (Mr. K, for short) tried his best to teach me the sciences. He was a retired footballer, a huge and no-nonsense kind of man who managed the whole classroom, maybe even the whole science wing, with his eyes. If they were focused in your direction, you immediately sat up straight and paid close attention. He never raised his voice, never threatened, and he was probably a very kind and caring man. Somehow, he was able to summon an appreciation of the complexities of physics and chemistry that helps me appreciate all that I don't know or understand. I trust that others who are far more capable are using this knowledge for the good of our planet.

I also remember Miss Pew (Ma Pew), a very experienced Biology teacher who not only gave me an appreciation for the complexity and order of life, but also the importance of keeping my binders organized.

Mr. Smiley taught grade twelve English in last period on Friday afternoons. He would start the class by loosening his tie, perch on a desk, and say, "I'm tired. Let's just talk. What do you think about…?" My English marks that year were higher than any other year spent with more formal instruction.

The ever-smiling Frau Blau always wore a blue dress and tried her best to teach me the complexities of French and German grammar. Mr. Pippy looked old enough to us to have personally experienced the history he tried to get us excited about.

These were the sixties. We listened to the Beatles, the Rolling Stones, Dave Clark Five, and so many more. A few of the bravest boys let their hair grow over their ears, and even down to their collars, much to the shock of the establishment. Denim was still considered work clothes, so we weren't allowed to wear jeans to school. Mostly, we wore pleated skirts and sweaters, but also woollen dress pants that needed sharply ironed creases. Skirts got consistently shorter as the decade wore on. We'd sleep on painful brush rollers to curl our hair into a flip, and we'd tease it to get lots of volume. Later, it was long straight hair; I required an iron and ironing board to achieve "the look."

Monday mornings, classmates would brag about how they crossed over to Buffalo, New York, to go drinking. The drinking age for us was twenty-one. Drugs like LSD were talked about, but I wasn't part of that culture and didn't know anyone who was.

The sixties were also the time of protest. I remember, and was a part of, students all gathering in the high school hallways to protest some offence, demanding to be heard and see change. The administration came to listen before scurrying back to the safety of their offices, and they tried to walk the fine line between satisfying the students enough without acceding control. I don't think we were protesting anything major—more likely some new "oppressive" school rule or the offerings in the cafeteria.

So much happened in that decade. President Kennedy's assassination shocked our world. I do remember where I was when I first heard. Martin Luther King and the fight for Civil Rights was getting a lot of media attention. We celebrated Neil Armstrong and Buzz Aldrin's small step onto the moon's surface as a giant leap for mankind. These were inspiring, culture-changing events that we lived through. Since we didn't have television at home, they were a bit less front and centre in my life, but they were nonetheless very influential.

We also changed churches then, leaving the Hamilton congregation where we were charter members and joining a larger sister congregation that had many more young people. The first Sunday we attended, a beautiful blond girl came up to me and said, "You must be about my age. We'll be friends!" That's how I met my teenage best friend, Hilda Bremer.

*Hilda. We had many fun adventures together as we enjoyed our teen years.*

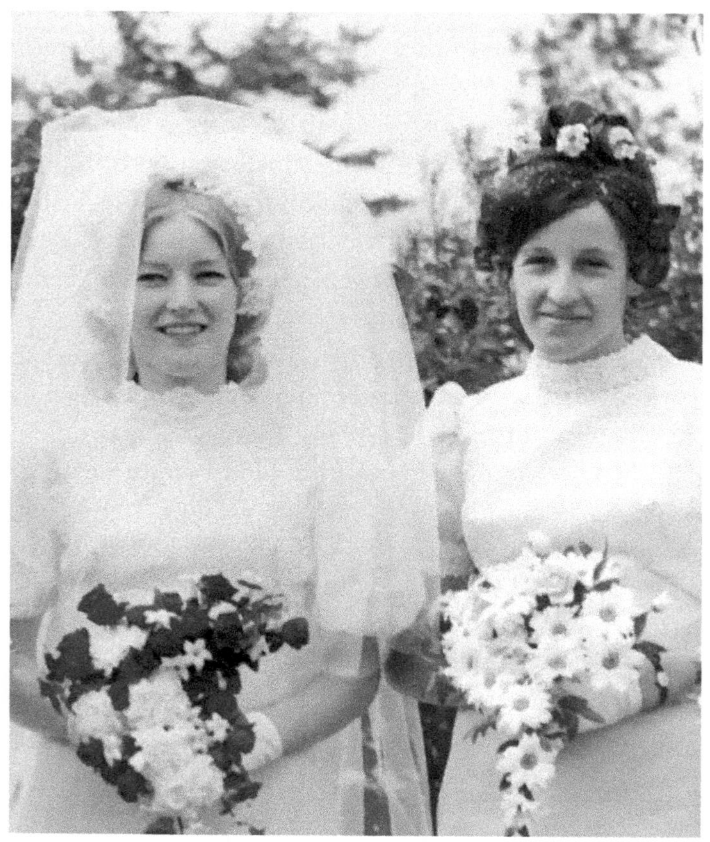

*I was maid of honour for Hilda.*

For many years, we did everything together outside of school. She went to the rival high school in town, but that didn't stop us. Hilda and I spent our Sundays together, alternating between her house and mine. Saturdays, if we got our chores done on time, we'd find a way to get together. I had a hard time figuring out how my Mom and I could get all of our chores done by noon in our larger house, while Hilda and her four sisters would need the whole day. Weeknights, we were often together at Catechism or Young-Young Peoples or Choir. Otherwise, we talked on the phone. We had a fair bit of freedom, since Hilda's Mom thought I was responsible and would keep her daughter grounded. We didn't abuse that too much, but we did have a lot of fun. My parents were also pretty trusting.

Sundays, we would take turns going to each other's house for lunch between church services, and maybe also for dinner. Many Sunday evenings would find us babysitting for a church family. Of course, being Sunday, we couldn't get paid, so it provided an affordable evening out for a young family. Some people would put out a few snacks for us, but mostly, and preferably, it would be, "Help yourself to whatever you would like." If they had a television set, it was a real bonus. For a while, I was 'dating' one of Hilda's brothers, and she was 'dating' one of mine. Sometimes we would have our brothers drop in and join us, and then, when the parents returned, we would say that they had just come to pick us up to save the parents from having to drive us home. I don't know if we fooled anyone.

When not babysitting, Hilda and I loved to go out for a walk. We would amble along the main streets and see how many whistles we could get, or maybe even have a car with cute boys stop for a chat with us. However, whenever they did, we hightailed it out of there pretty quickly, giggling all the way.

As we got a bit older, fifteen or sixteen, we would get together with more friends and chat and giggle, listen to the hit parade songs, and play silly games. Sunday hikes in our miniskirts and heels were an adventure as well. We were discouraged from changing out of our Sunday clothes, so we learned to do a lot of things in our skirts. Boys went ahead when we had to climb, and they offered us a gallant hand up.

Sunday evenings, the church youth liked to gather together, and since we had a large living room and a big yard to allow for baseball or Twenty-One- Up, my brothers and I often found ourselves hosting. We would come home from church and tell my parents that they needed to go out for the evening, and then the house would fill up with twenty to thirty young people. We drank coffee, served the rest of the Sunday baking, and played silly games or got into interesting discussions. We had a lot of fun together.

Many of the girls my age quit school at sixteen, including my best friend, Hilda. You could graduate with a junior matriculation and get into a business college or a nursing assistant program, or you could go straight into the workforce. These girls were out working and earning pretty young. And that's what the thinking was. In a few years, they'd probably be married and staying home to have babies, so any further education would be wasted, and the money they could save or contribute to their families in those years would be very helpful.

I was too young to quit after Grade ten, and by the time I turned sixteen, I was almost done grade twelve. I'd always wanted to be a teacher, and if I pushed through Grade thirteen and one year of Teacher's College, I could achieve my goal and still be working by the time I was eighteen. So that's what I did. I accepted my first job, teaching grade five at John Calvin School in Burlington. This was the school set up and operated by parents from my church.

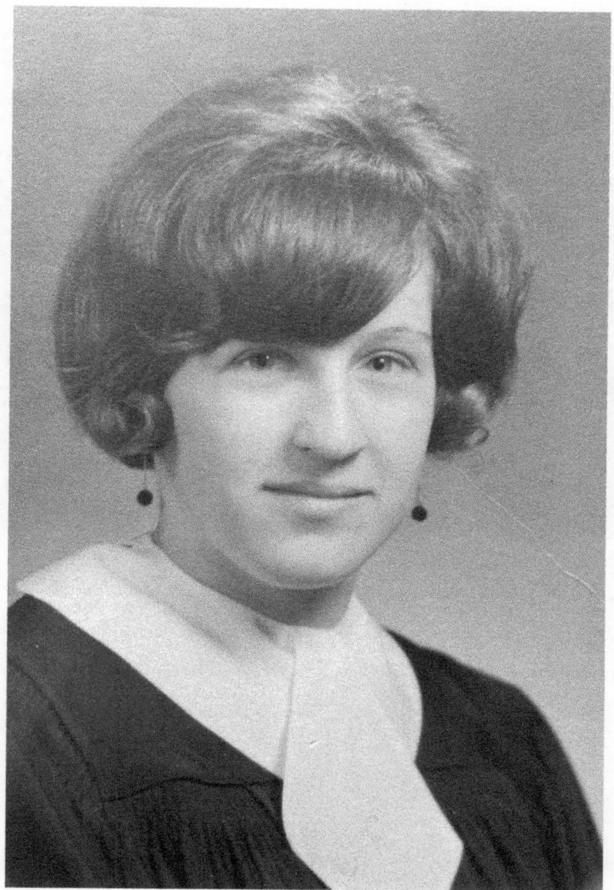

*Graduation from Hamilton Teacher's College 1968*

The teens were good years. My circle expanded as friendships became a bigger part of my life, and there were so many new things to experience and learn. These years are about questioning and pushing boundaries and growing toward independence as we begin to develop our own identity, and I did all of these.

*The family 1967. Mom and Dad are in the front with Grace and John's three children, Sonja, Sidney and Bradley. Back LtoR: Little Johnny, Harry, Grace, Big Johnny (VanderWoude), Fran, Margaret, Ben, Diane, Jane (Herman's fiancé), and Herman.*

# CHAPTER 12

## Faith: It's Complicated

My simple childlike faith grew and developed through my teenage struggles. I became aware of the teaching of election, that God chooses some people, people like us, but that there are others that God doesn't reveal Himself to, so they miss out on salvation. This seemed so unfair, cruel and unlike the God I had learned to trust. I struggled so much with this, even to the point of wondering if I had to throw my faith away altogether, since I couldn't trust an imperfect or unloving God. It was all or nothing. But I also couldn't walk away. I spent hours worrying about this and probably discussing it with my friends. It helped a bit when our pastor, Rev VanDooren, said that we were not "chosen to be saved from hell" but chosen to spread the gospel, to make God known. But the need to understand and work it out became stronger and stronger.

After completing the traditional Catechism instruction at eighteen years old and being examined by the Church

Consistory, I was allowed, along with my classmates, to make Public Profession or Confession of Faith in a special worship service. This was an important transition that called for a new dress, and even a hat! (Neither of these were obligatory, but it was a good excuse nonetheless.) I was now allowed to participate in Lord's Supper or Communion. If I had been a male, I would also have been given a vote at Congregational meetings, but now I had to be content to be represented by my Dad. And I could be hired on as a teacher in John Calvin School, since teachers needed to be confessing members of the Church.

There was a group of us that asked our pastor, Rev VanDooren, if we could do a post-confession class to dig a bit deeper. He agreed and taught us some of what he taught in his first-year seminary preaching classes. One of these was about reading and understanding the Scriptures in a historic redemptive context.

The Bible is the story of how we, as humankind, struggled with whom we were (and are) and how we are to live by faith, following in the ways of Jesus. And we can best understand it when we place each book in its historic and cultural context, trying to discern what the original, intended audience would have heard and understood in that particular circumstance. One of those cultural influences would have been understanding ourselves not as individuals, but always within the community—part of a family, tribe, and nation. Individual faith and a personal relationship with God are a more recent concept of the modern age, and they influence how we read and interpret Scripture. This was all so interesting and helpful to me, especially as I was just beginning my teaching career.

My teen years were, as expected and required for growth in maturity, marked by questions and struggles. I had been well trained by Mr. Haddon back in elementary school to continually ask, "Why?" It made life more challenging but so much richer. Emerging from the simple, uncomplicated blacks and whites of childhood, I was exposed to grey areas. As I delved into them, I discovered that they are not really greys—they are all the colours, shades, and tints of the rainbow. It has taken all of my adult life to become aware of these colours and learn to appreciate how they all are important and beautiful, and how they fit together to make the intricate patterns and pictures of wholeness and truth.

# ADULTHOOD

# CHAPTER 13

## Holland (1969)

In many ways, graduating from school and beginning your first job is an entry into adulthood. My parents had made that transition at twelve years old. I was eighteen. Legally, at the time, you were considered an adult at twenty-one. In reality, it's a process that takes a long time. I was well into my twenties before I felt like I had a small clue about what I was doing, and I sometimes still feel like I'm not a whole lot further. I just don't get as stressed about it, recognizing that no-one knows everything; we all make lots of mistakes and learn by trying. In the end, it's about living and loving.

I taught fifth grade at John Calvin School for my first year and saved enough of the meagre dollars I earned to buy a ticket on a three-week charter flight to Holland. This was an important dream for me to connect with my roots, getting to know the people that were mostly stories, and seeing the villages, towns, and country of my birth. My parents were very excited for me to be able to do this as well.

I stayed with Dad's brother, Oom GJ, and Tante Liny. Their youngest sons, twins Bertus and Jan, were a few years older than my nineteen, and they were still living at home. They were built-in Dutch language tutors and tour guides. We had so much fun together.

*My home in Holland on the Hessenweg.*

Next door, the Odinks had a number of teens and young adult kids, and next door to them, my beloved Tante Fenna

(Mom's younger sister) and Oom Freek lived with their fun-loving family of seven surviving children. They had lost three children in infancy to a genetic disease that sounded a lot like the spinal muscular atrophy my nephew Pieter had.

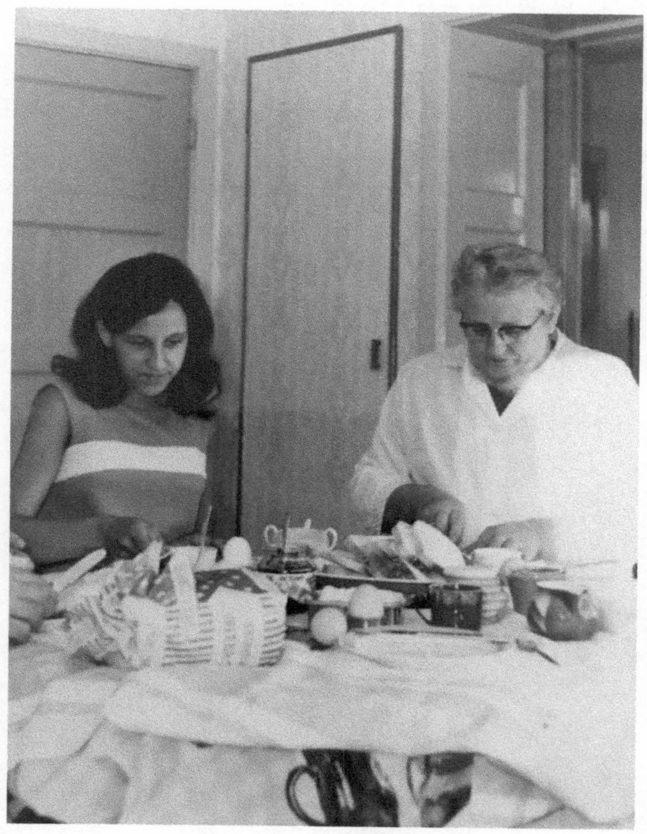

*Tante Liny and I enjoying a meal.*

My uncle, Oom Barts, was on his deathbed with cancer (though they never would tell them what it was, for cancer wasn't talked about out loud). The one and only time I got to meet him was a week before he died, and he welcomed me with the gentleness of a beloved family member. The next week, I walked in the rainy procession that carried his body, in a horse-drawn carriage, from the church to the cemetery. In the sea of black, I felt quite out of place in my lime-green all-weather coat, but it was all I had.

Opa and Opoe, whom I had met when they came to visit us back in 1958, lived in with their youngest son, Oom Evert, Tante Jenny, and their young family. I so envied those kids for having grandparents right there every day. I now also got to spend afternoons sitting with them, sharing a meal at their table, and enjoying their company.

*Two Fennys!*

This trip to the land of my birth was such a special time in my life. I learned to speak and understand Dutch so much better. After a few weeks there, I even found myself dreaming in Dutch. I met all my aunts and uncles and many cousins.

I also got to experience biking everywhere. I had parked my bike when I was about twelve years old because bikes were for kids back in the sixties. But now, as I biked behind my hefty aunt going into town to run errands, I was trying to restrain my laughter, picturing what this would look like in my hometown of Burlington. Longer trips were by train, but the trip to and from the train station was made sitting on the back of my cousin's bike, balancing my suitcase as he pedalled through the main streets. My uncle did have a car, a little Daf, but he didn't have a driver's licence, so Bertus and Jan got to chauffeur them around. We also occasionally got to use it to tour the country.

Holland was a bit more conservative than we were at the time. I wore Bermuda shorts. They wore dresses. I shaved my underarms. They didn't. I was the talk of the town! Yet, when we went to the beach, the girls stripped off their dresses to reveal pretty tiny bikinis, while I was still used to one-piece or conservative two-piece swimsuits. When it came to beach food, I had no trouble giving up our typical pop and hot dogs in favour of sausages and croquettes.

I loved the sense of history in Holland. History came alive when I walked down streets that were hundreds of years old, and was told by a cousin that King So-and-So of England had lived in that house back about five hundred years ago when he had to flee. The house was still there and still lived in.

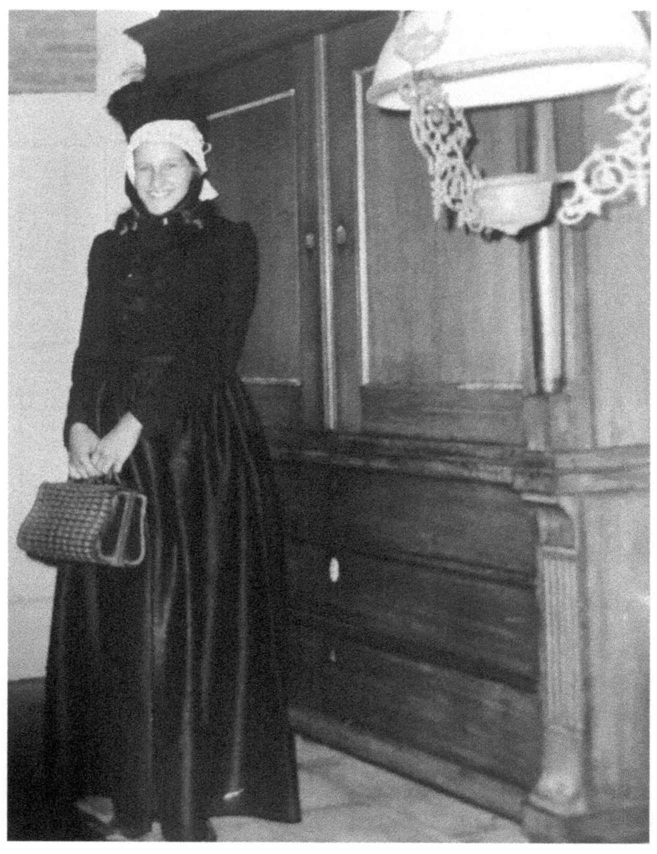

*Dress up day.*

Visiting museums like the Open-Air Museum in Arnhem or the Veen Museum in Orfelte brought Dutch history to life. And so did places like Schevening, Staphorst, and Urk, where people could still be seen wearing the traditional Dutch clothing as they went about their day. And, of course, we visited Holten, the Cemetery and Memorial where so many young Canadian soldiers were buried.

When I was there, you could still see the old ways alongside the new, emerging Holland. I could stare out of my aunt's front window and see elderly people biking by in their traditional dress and milk cans being taken on a horse-drawn cart to the dairy. I visited another aunt and uncle in their old home, where their farm consisted of scattered plots in the area, just before they moved to a new farm where all their land and buildings were on one property. Old-style farms, like Oom Barts and Tante Hendrikje's, where the barn was attached to the house were still in use, but some were already being renovated into beautiful modern homes.

The time spent here allowed me to understand myself and my identity so much better. I was welcomed with open hearts and arms by Ooms, Tantes, and cousins I'd only ever heard about. I drank it all in greedily. As I enjoyed time with my cousins, I thought that this could have been me. And I realized two things: first, I had roots, place, and an honourable, rich, and loving heritage, and second, I was glad my parents had taken us to Canada.

In Canada, I always felt like I was the newcomer who didn't quite get the culture and was hesitant to fully join in unless it was in our immigrant church community. In Holland, I felt like I belonged, like these were people who accepted and understood me. Yet, Holland needed to develop and prosper. Holland's long history made it more challenging to bring about change. Social hierarchies and faith alliances were bred deep into the bone of each person, and it would take much time and intentional effort to bring about new ways. So many memories, customs, and traditions were closely intertwined with the land. The villages and extended family connections made the need to change less obvious and more challenging.

Canada, with its shorter history and its mishmash of immigrant groups, saw itself as a land of opportunity, and it was more strategically set up to move forward. In some ways, as an immigrant community, we were still living in the past identity of being Dutch in the 1950s. In other ways, we were living and working within more diverse neighbourhoods, and we had to think things through for ourselves. I had learned to appreciate the freedom of having a past, but not being bound by looking back at it. We had changed and adapted in so many ways just by moving to a new place and having to figure things out on our own, or within an immigrant church community that consisted of people from all over the Netherlands. While Canadian society also had its socioeconomic layers, we were free, expected, and encouraged, to move onwards and upwards.

*Me enjoying the photo album cousin Bertus put together as a farewell gift for me.*

# CHAPTER 14

## Teaching, Part One (1968–1971)

When I was eighteen, John Calvin School hired me to teach the grade five class. This was a private Christian school operated by parents from our local church community. Johnny, Diane and Margaret all went to this school. Diane was in Grade 8, and Margaret was in Grade 7when I taught there but I don't really remember having much contact with them at school.

I was terrified, especially that first day. I still felt like a kid, so it was challenging to make the transition of seeing myself "on the other side" as a teacher. Calling teachers by their first names took real effort. I didn't feel like a Miss Harsevoort at all. Yet, there I was, doing my best to bluff my way through.

I soon learned the names and began to know the personalities of each of the thirty-three students, and they started to feel like my family. We developed our relationships and routines, and day-by-day, it got a bit easier. I had two cousins in my class, Harry and Teresa. I was so thankful for them, as they seemed particularly sympathetic. Teresa could sing like an angel, and I had difficulty carrying a tune in a bucket so I asked her to teach new songs, which she graciously did.

The school was operated on funds contributed by immigrant families that were all still struggling to establish themselves. The pay was low, especially for the single women, and we had very little in the way of resources. I had a class set of old math texts, readers, and maybe spellers. Each child had their Bible and Book of Praise. For the rest, it was a mishmash of a few copies of discarded language, science, or social studies books. The only "curriculum" consisted of the list of Bible books to be covered in each grade. I would go regularly to the public library and borrow a big box of books on my teacher's card to stock our classroom library. And I had the sets of encyclopaedias I had gotten a good deal on in Teacher's College.

The professional support consisted of the principal saying, "If you have any questions, come and ask me." But we were each expected to be self-sufficient behind the closed doors of our own classrooms. There were no staff meetings. There were no professional development opportunities like attending conferences or exploring curriculums. The Christian Schools were beginning to develop their own resources and have conferences, but we were not allowed to use these. The devil wore clunky wooden shoes in the secular materials but slid in on slippers in the "Christian" resources. It was important to retain our own identity as a liberated church and school. So, we did the best we could.

The expectation was to have quiet, obedient children sitting up straight in orderly rows, soaking up the knowledge and wisdom of the teacher at the front. To be fair, the school board members were mostly elementary school graduates back in Holland, and the principal had little more than the one-year teachers' college.

Parents often assured me that if their child gave me any trouble, I was free to punish them, and the parent would probably punish them again when they found out about it.

The highlight of my day was the daily Bible lesson. For thirty minutes at the start of the day, we would all open our Bibles and take turns reading through the chapters. Have you read the Bible through the eyes of a child? These ten- to fourteen-year-olds knew their Bibles quite well by fifth grade, and they were able to make connections between stories that amazed me. They also had not yet been taught the doctrines of the Creeds and Confessions, so they took the words of the Bible at face value. I am so thankful for the privilege I had in being able to read the Bible through children's eyes for fourteen years. It has forever shaped how I read those verses. Sometimes, I would get the questions like, "Teacher, if Jesus said…, why do we…?" Sometimes, I would try to answer, but mostly I had to just acknowledge and ponder.

I loved those kids. I loved learning along with them. Years later, I was seeing them filling a church bench with their own children, who looked so much like them. Some of the boys were now men (or "big boys" to me), sitting up among the elders and deacons. They all happily chatted with me after church. I got so much out of teaching; it laid a strong foundation for my adult life.

# CHAPTER 15

## Faith: Making It Personal

I was not very good at making sure that the kids sat still and listened obediently. My classroom was often rowdy and looked unorganized as we learned and grew together—a recurring theme in my life. So, in February of my third year, the principal informed me that my contract would not be renewed and that in his, and presumably the Board's, opinion I should look for another career because I was obviously not cut out to be a teacher.

I was devastated. Totally devastated. Since first grade I had wanted to be a teacher, and now I was being told that I didn't have it in me. My world fell apart. To add to the blow, a guy I had been "very good friends" with and had dated on and off for two or three years broke up with me. My life was over and I was not quite twenty-one. It may sound melodramatic, but it was true to me. I had no career left and no prospect of marriage, since all the good guys had already been taken by this age. I had no hope. Yet, I still had to get up each morning and teach my class until the end of the school year four long months away. I don't know how I did it. I know my family ached for me. And my friends were great. But it was hard to talk about it.

That Easter, my friends convinced me to go to the annual study weekend that the provincial Church Young People's groups organized. So, with no better options, I agreed to go. During the formal speech (the study part of the weekend), the pastor spoke about how God knew each of us and had a plan for us. (I'm still not sure if that's what he said or if that's what I heard, but it doesn't matter.) My faith had always been real, and especially since I was teaching in the church school, my whole life was in the "Christian bubble." Yet, on this day, this message hit me like a wrecking ball.

My first response was a deep sense of shame and grief. "God, I've known you all my life, thought of and called myself a Christian, yet I've never intentionally asked you what I should be doing. I've just tried to figure it out by myself." I felt so ashamed. And yet, the flip side of that page was that I *could*. I could ask God, and he would answer me specifically. He saw *me*. God knew *me*. And God wanted to work together on a plan specific to *me*.

I was blown away. I wasn't valued just because I belonged to the multitude of the church as long as I stayed within its walls. I was actually seen, known, and loved by God! I don't know why it took me so long to figure this out, and I'm sure I knew, and hopefully even taught it. But it was just what I needed in my time of despair.

I can't describe how I felt at the time other than to use the "walking on cloud nine" analogy. In a moment, my frame shifted from despair to joy and confidence. And I promised

God that never again would I make a decision without talking it over with Him. Fifty years later, I can say that I'm still walking on that cloud, and I've made all my life's decisions based on going forward only in the confidence that God is with me, going before me. It is a cloud. Not a rock. It doesn't always feel very secure and stable. You can't see very far—usually just enough to be able to place your next step. You can maybe see vague shapes in the distance, sometimes more clearly than others. Sounds are also somewhat muted and softened. It is being enveloped in the love and wisdom of an all-knowing and all-powerful God.

God gave me tangible proof that my life was not over yet. I got hired at Calvin Christian School in Dundas, a half-hour commute from home. I also started a relationship with another friend. Both this young man and I had just experienced painful breakups, and we were not ready to risk emotional attachment, so we agreed to be good friends and have fun. And we did have so many good times for the next six months or so.

# CHAPTER 16

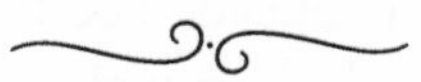

## Teaching, Part Two (1971--1982)

I spent eight wonderful years teaching in the Christian School in Dundas. This was such a welcoming community. It was a rural school where the kids came from farm or small business families that needed them to help out. When they were at school, they relished the time to learn and play, and they were friendly and polite. It amazed me and every visitor at the school.

We had regular staff meetings, district meetings, and an annual conference. The other staff members were welcoming and happy to share their knowledge and experiences. And there were resources, actual curriculums, and books. It was also a treat to be still inside the Christian Bubble, though a slightly larger and more flexible one, where I was seen and appreciated as a professional teacher. Then I could go to my home community and church and just be me. So, yes, I was cut out to teach. And I loved it.

Eight years later, I left this lovely community to return to my first school. They were experiencing a severe teacher shortage because they could only hire members of our church denomination. I thought that after eight years I would have enough confidence and strength to go back. How hard could it be?

It was hard. Very hard. Many days, I felt like walking out, and one day I did. You see, not much had changed. The staff was cliquey, and I was on the outside because I was tainted through my Christian school teaching experience. I wasn't really one of them anymore. That might have been bearable, but not much work had been done as far as the resources and curriculum went. I took along my lesson plans from Dundas and used those where I could, but I was told that I needed to use a recently developed curriculum for social studies. The problem was that it was worse than useless. It looked like someone had copied the titles of chapters of a textbook without giving the name of the book. And that was all I was given. I asked the principal if we could use an upcoming professional development day to discuss the social studies program and how it transitioned through the grades. "I'm willing to introduce it," I naively said.

So, that morning, I presented some of my ideas on what social studies were about and how we could potentially deal with it in a Christian worldview. When I was done, the others either remained quiet or started to pick holes in it. I didn't mind the scrutiny, since my goal was to get a good product at the end of the day, so asked what they would suggest instead. They had no suggestions, but many more criticisms. Soon, I realized that all I believed and tried to do in my classroom had been judged to be wrong, and nothing was suggested as an alternative.

When we broke for lunch, I fled in tears and didn't return that day. That evening, I sobbed to the Board Chair that I couldn't go back on Monday because I had nothing left to teach. And that's exactly how I felt. She was a calm and wise woman, and she assured me that I should go back and that the Board would back me.

Monday morning, the teacher who had led the attack came into my room and apologized, which I was happy to accept. And the Board followed through, using the opportunity to do a thorough evaluation of the system and create conversations to develop a new vision and plans. I became staff liaison to the Board. My colleagues abandoned their cliques and became open to thinking in new ways, and the school began to change. I ended up teaching there for three more years, and we had a lot of fun and made a lot of progress.

I had wanted to be a teacher since first grade. My teaching career was a rollercoaster ride, but I can think of no better career to learn life lessons and leadership skills. It is emotionally and spiritually challenging and fulfilling.

# CHAPTER 17

## My Twenties

*Mom and I making sure everyone is well fed.*

The twenties are an awkward age. We are expected to be adults, but there is so much we don't know about what that entails. So, we do our best to "fake it until we make it." My siblings and many of my friends got engaged and married in their early twenties, so they had someone else to "grow up together" with. It probably didn't make it any easier for them, but it looked like more fun to me. The path was laid out for them. Get married, have babies, buy a house, raise your family. This was the norm, so you had lots of companionship and support along the way from fellow church and community members.

I was single. This caused many people to wonder, and sometimes even ask me, "What's wrong with you, that you're not married yet?" Truth be told, I often asked myself that same question, so I won't pass judgment on them.

Some people thought I was just too independent. When I got my driver's licence and bought my first car, a male friend stated that I would now probably not get married because I was no longer dependent on the guys with wheels to give me a ride home.

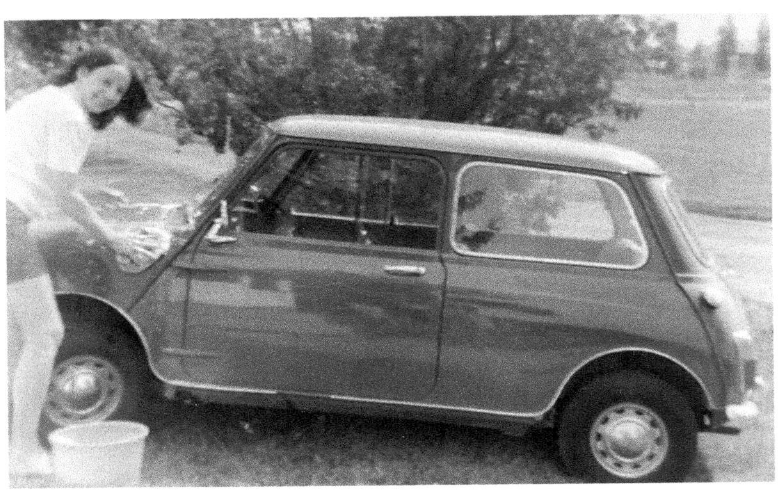

*My pride and joy. My brothers made me a silver wind-up-key that suctioned to the roof for my birthday. I had so much fun with my first car.*

As friends got married and went down the typical family journey, I found that I had less and less in common with them. There were always new friends to make, however, and I found interesting people who also didn't fit the most common life pattern.

I had my opportunities to get married. But I had always known pretty early in a relationship whether I wanted to continue it or not. And, after my face-to-face encounter with God at age twenty-one, I had promised Him, and myself, that I wouldn't make decisions without being sure that this was God's will for me. So, each time, I chose to remain in the teaching career that I loved. I sometimes could picture myself living alone in a small, cozy home with lots of plants and a cat or two.

I moved out of the house to share a lovely four-bedroom apartment with three other teachers. It was actually a home built above a small plaza. We called it our penthouse. It was a lot of fun and a good time to gain greater independence and skills in things like cooking and household management. We had friends dropping in regularly, and we built some really good relationships. Friday evenings, my friend Janey's little portable stereo would be blasting the Beatles' "Ob-La-di Ob-La-Da," and we would feel the stresses and tensions of the week melt away as we sang and danced along.

It was a privilege to be able to walk beside others as they were also living the realities of life. There was much to celebrate and explore. There were also some very difficult and dark times for many of us. As we learned to become more vulnerable with one another, we were able to help each other and also to grow in wisdom and empathy ourselves.

Of course, one by one, they got married or moved away, and new friends moved in. But, eventually, after four years, I decided to move back home.

*This is me around 1980.*

I love to travel. My first year's salary went to paying for a trip back to the land of my birth. Five years later, I returned to Holland, this time with my friend and roommate, Janey. We spent three weeks in Holland, visiting my relatives and hers. She came from a very different part of Holland—Goeree Overflakee, an island just south of Rotterdam. Then we strapped on our backpacks, got out our Eurorail passes, and set off to explore western Europe. Arthur Frommer's *Europe on $10 a Day* gave us lots of recommendations for affordable accommodations and places to eat, as well as highlighting must-see sights, the known and the hidden, in each place. We set off on a long train ride to Paris to see its gems.

Next, we headed down to Spain. Spain had its own rail system that was a slightly different size and far less efficient than the rest of Europe, so it meant transferring to a Spanish train, long delays, and less comfortable seating than the first class our Eurorail Pass had us accustomed to. However, the people were very friendly as we bounced along toward Sitges for a few days on the beach. A stop in Barcelona allowed us to become more familiar with Picasso, and then we continued on to Rome.

Being naïve and cautious travellers, we carried traveller's cheques. Their downside is that they could best be exchanged for cash at a bank. We arrived in the main train station in Rome late on a Saturday evening with nary an Italian lira in our pockets. We were hooped. We couldn't use a phone to call a hotel, board a bus, or hire a taxi. We couldn't even pee, since you had to pay the attendants to use the facilities. Two handsome young off-duty soldiers approached us with offers to help. They found us a hotel, took us by bus, and made sure we were safe. We were so grateful. We made plans to meet up with them later in the week, but unfortunately, while we were in our rooms waiting for them, the hotel clerk said that we had gone out. I still feel badly about standing them up.

Rome was so lovely. I loved how they live with, and in, their history. The people were very friendly—the men, especially, but that wasn't always a good thing. We visited St. Peter's Basilica and the Vatican Museum. The Sistine Chapel was mesmerizing. We visited as many of the well known historical, cultural, and religious sights as we could crowd into our few days there. Rome held romantic surprises, such as a free ballet performance in a park, where the performers danced to music played on a box record player.

From Rome, we went to Florence, feasting on Michelangelo and other great artists. Then, it was off to Innsbruck, then Switzerland, where we hit the highlights, including a few days listening to Francis Schaeffer at L'Abri. Finally, a cruise up the Rhine brought us to Koln, and then it was a short trip back to Holland. It was thirty days of absorbing so much history and culture. It was exhausting but so enriching. We took rolls and rolls of film, had them printed into slides, and were able to share some of our adventures with our students and friends.

In 1979, another five years later, I went to Holland, this time with my cousin Teresa. I had taught her back in my first year, and she was the angel who helped me with the music. Now, she was all grown up and a dear friend. Precious memories were made as I reconnected with aunts, uncles, and cousins that were now more familiar to me.

I also toured my home country, Canada. A group of us drove across to the west coast one summer. With four drivers, we could cover a lot of road. The first leg was a twenty-six-hour drive to Winnipeg. As soon as we saw the sign "Welcome to Winnipeg," we pulled over to the shoulder and slept for a few hours before finding a campsite. Catching the RCMP Musical Ride in Regina, Saskatchewan, ended with sharing a beer with some young recruits.

We looked up friends in Calgary and Edmonton, and then we drove to Jasper. My first experience of being in the beautiful Rocky Mountains was just overwhelming. Such grandeur! I felt very small, yet very much a part of the vastness.

Finally, we reached the Fraser Valley and spent a few weeks sightseeing and making friends. We had sister church congregations here, so it was a good way to connect. When we attended a church service, we were sure to be invited over for a coffee by someone, and the young people there were always eager to extend hospitality and make new friends,

Another summer, we took the shorter, but no less magnificent, trip to the east coast. The old city of Quebec, with its Street of the Artists and so much history, felt a lot like Europe. The pastoral beauty of New Brunswick, small towns nestled in the valleys, each with its steepled church anchoring its centre, were a delight to drive through. We were amazed at the beauty of Nova Scotia, especially its picturesque fishing villages. And, of course, tiny, lovely PEI had its own charm. We were able to take in Anne of Green Gables as live Theatre in the Charlottetown Confederation Centre and visit the home of Lucy Maud Montgomery. We learned to love fresh lobster.

Yet another summer, we headed to northern Ontario. Camping beside northern lakes, listening to the loons and the wolves call back and forth across the lake, was pure magic. Since the roads didn't go further, we took the train, the Polar Bear Express, from Cochrane, through miles of dense forest up, to Moose Factory.

We have such a beautiful and diverse country. The land, the people—I'm so proud to be a part of it!

My twenties were full of diverse experiences. I found time to take university courses, learn to ski, make new friends, travel, and so much more. I remained involved in church, being part of Bible Studies and the Evangelism committee. But I also began stepping outside when I became active in what was initially called Burlington Right to Life, and later was rebranded as Halton Pro-Life. I learned so much under the mentorship of these visionary mostly Roman Catholic, people, and it was my first foray into the community and political arena. They were good years where I gained knowledge, confidence, and independence.

# CHAPTER 18

## Very Difficult Times: Siena Harsevoort-Hutten, April 1, 1918- Nov 12, 1980

I was privileged to be able to help my parents buy a nicer home—a comfortable brick bungalow back in Aldershot that was near to many of the married siblings' homes. With only Margaret and I still living at home, we no longer needed the old large house. This new home was bright and easy to keep clean. We used the opportunity to buy new furniture as well. Mom was so happy here. She got much pleasure from finally having nice stuff. She had made the best of it for so many years, always putting her family first before her own needs and desires. She worked so hard and never complained, finding joy in seeing her family happy. Now, she was able to afford a few nice things and buy some new outfits and home decorations. She was very happy with them, and I was thankful and delighted to see and share her joy.

When Dad reached sixty-five, he retired from his role as Head Caretaker at Mary Hopkins School in Waterdown. Now, they had time for the leisurely drives Mom always loved so much. Visits with their children, grandchildren, and relatives were always top priority, but they also enjoyed many coffees and chats with friends. They had had dreams of travelling, back to Holland for an extended vacation with their families. They even thought of going off to British Columbia to visit friends in far-away Smithers and spend time in the magnificent mountains. They did make a three-week visit to Holland.

I was especially thankful for all of this when Mom was diagnosed with cancer in the spring of 1980.

April 1980 was such a horrible month. While Mom was in hospital recovering from surgery and adjusting to a terminal cancer diagnosis, my sister-in-law, Janet (my little brother John's wife), had a cardiac arrest. Mom was in Burlington's Joseph Brant Hospital. Dad and I were asleep when I was awakened by a voice outside my bedroom window. "Can you go and open up the front door?" Groggily, I got up and started for the door when I woke up enough to go back and ask who was there. It was my brother-in-law, Big Johnny, who had come to tell us that Janet had had a cardiac arrest and was also in Joseph Brant Hospital. Neither Dad nor I had heard the telephone's repeated rings, so they had had to come wake us up. We spent the rest of that night in the hospital hallway outside her room, anxiously waiting to hear how she was. We wheeled Mom down in her wheelchair a few days later.

She was one of the few to survive a cardiac arrest outside of hospital. This was her second serious event in her long and courageous struggle with heart disease. About fifteen years later, she underwent a heart transplant, then a kidney transplant, and lived long enough to see her sons all grow up. Unfortunately, she also lived long enough to experience the death of her firstborn son in a construction accident. That, she said, was harder than anything she had had to endure. Her faith was so strong and real.

I flew out to visit her a bit before her heart transplant, and as I was leaving her room, she called me back and said, "Fran, whether I live or die isn't important to me. I want nothing more than to be with Jesus. But I also want to be here for John and the boys." A few years after her transplant, when she was doing quite well again, she reminded me of that conversation and then said, "I want you to know that nothing has changed!"

Also, around the same time, my cousin-brother Gerry plummeted from some scaffolding, landed on his head, and broke many bones in his face. He did make a complete recovery, thankfully. They were dark and anxious days, and the family grew even closer.

*Mom, 1978.*

Meanwhile Mom was struggling with her failing health and cancer. For the past six months or so, she had been noticing that she was losing a lot of weight, and she could not eat very well. She'd be hungry and happily sit down to a delicious meal, but then, after a few bites, she couldn't eat any more. Doctor's visits and tests didn't show anything wrong, so she tried her best to keep going, but it didn't get better. Finally, after many months, her doctor sent her for an endoscopy. Again, nothing. However, that night, she was feeling particularly awful and began throwing up blood, so I took her to the Emergency Room at Joseph Brant Hospital. They immediately performed emergency surgery and discovered cancer on the stomach. It was too advanced to remove, so they closed her up again and estimated that she would have about six months to live.

Mom was given the choice to have chemotherapy, but was told that it would, at best, give her a few more months. She struggled with it, wondering if it was her duty to prolong her life as long as possible. In the end, she decided that God didn't require that, and she would prefer to spend those days living a better quality of life with her family. She was calm and accepting that she would die, at least she appeared calm on the outside. I'm sure she went through many conflicting emotions, including all the stages of grieving and reflecting on life. But she was a private person who processed much of this within her own heart, along with Dad and her pastor, Rev. Pouwelse, who visited her often.

Dad became her primary care giver. I was living at home with them and teaching in Burlington. As she got weaker, Dad waited on her hand and foot. He did the cleaning and grocery shopping, cooked all the meals, and made sure that she was always comfortable. He doted on her as he had done all their married life. She had truly always been the love of his life.

When he would recall courting her, he would get all choked up, recalling how beautiful she was to him then and still always was. And she had always been his strong support.

I'm sure they had many conversations starting with, "When I am gone…" She, who knew him so well, worried about him; they walked through death together. "Make sure that you visit the kids regularly. Take along some chocolate bars for the grandkids. Don't sit alone, you'll get depressed." And even, "It's okay to marry again."

The house was often full of visitors—family, of course. Her kids came to see her every day, and the grandkids came often. Extended family were regulars. And church members showed their love and respect for her in so many ways. Some came weekly to encourage her. Others, like my friend Bonnie, a nurse, dropped in regularly to keep a professional eye on her. And Dad made and poured coffee and tea, and he monitored the situation to ensure that she didn't overdo things.

*Tante Fenna, Oom Freek, Tante Janke, Uncle Gerry, Aunt Jane and Uncle John trying to squeeze into the photo standing behind Mom and Dad.*

Mom recovered enough to have her sister, Tante Fenna, and Oom Freek come from Holland to visit her that summer when they celebrated their fortieth wedding anniversary. She was already so thin and pale by then. I was thankful to be living at home to support both Mom and Dad through this hard time. Thankfully, she didn't have great pain. She described it as more of a miserable feeling, mostly. Toward the end, as her pain increased, it was fairly well managed with medication.

As she grew weaker, her circle grew more intimate. At first, she limited visitors to family, then in the final weeks, to her children only. She let go of her people one ring at a time.

We have always been close as siblings, but during those trying months, we were together every day and constantly checked in with one another on an emotional level.

She died November 12, 1980. I went into their bedroom in the morning before leaving for school to tell her, "Good morning," but she had quietly slipped away during the night, with Dad cuddled up next to her, sound asleep by her side. That was her style. Not alone, but also no drama.

That day, my sisters, brothers, and I often found ourselves gathering around the empty bed. It just felt less lonely there. Death creates holy space. She was there. I truly felt that she could see, hear, and love us. But we couldn't see her. She never got to meet my husband and children. Yet, I feel her presence and awareness even today. She's looking at us all with love. My husband and children never got to meet her, and that's the tragedy.

And that leads me to the next story.

# CHAPTER19

## Pieter Vanderpol

On Christmas Eve, 1980, my Aunt Jane called me. Forgive me for a bit of Dutch Bingo here, but it provides a bit of context. Aunt Jane, my Uncle John's wife, has a younger brother who lived in Surrey, BC, and was married to Ria Vanderpol. Ah! You're seeing a connection with the Vanderpol name. Aunt Jane had heard from Ria that Ria's brother, Pieter, his wife, Rika, and their children had been in a car accident on their way to Smithers to celebrate Christmas with relatives. Rika was killed almost immediately. That now left Pieter a widower with six children. "I think you know them," she said.

She was correct. Rika was the sister of my very good friend and former roommate, Janey VanDyk, now VanSeters. I had met Pieter and Rika a few times, first one weekend when they came to Ontario for a business trip, then when I journeyed westward for Janey's wedding, and later to visit her and admire her babies.

This was hard news to take. Having experienced grief and loss so recently myself, I had much empathy for Pieter and his kids. But—and here's a secret I will share with you now--while we were lamenting this a voice in my head suddenly said, "And you're going to marry him!" I was outraged! How could anyone even be thinking of those things in this heavy time of grief? But the voice just stubbornly stayed there until finally I said, "If that's you God, you'll have to make it happen. I'm not doing anything!"

I said nothing about it to anyone! And I tried my best to discredit and banish the thought from my mind.

During March break, I visited Janey again. After Rika's death, Janey had committed to maintaining close connections with Rika's kids and providing Pieter with a woman he could safely talk with by visiting them every week. So, when I was there, she took me along. Pieter was still mired in grief, but he was very intentionally trying to be both father and mother to his kids.

Fast forward to November, and the voice returned. Once in a while, as I would walk in the door after school, it would slyly suggest that there might be a letter waiting for me. There never was. I told the voice to go away and leave me alone.

Then, one day in January, the principal gave me a letter that had been addressed to me, using the school address. We were both kind of puzzled, and the address looked familiar, but didn't ring a bell. I took it into my empty classroom (it was lunch recess) to read it. My world changed once again. Pieter Vanderpol had written me a letter.

*Jan 15, 1982*

*Dear Frances,*

*It is a little more than a year ago that the Lord took Rika unto Himself. It has been a very long and difficult year for us, as I'm sure you'll understand, for you must have experienced the same when your mother passed away. We have had to make many adjustments and have wrestled with many questions, but the Lord has given us everything that we needed to make the necessary adjustments. He has also given me greater understanding in His ways, and the strength to continue the task that He has given me. However, because I am able to do it alone does not necessarily mean that it must continue this way. I would like to have another "help meet" for as many years as the Lord will give me, and although I know "that with His hand He still brings to every man his wife," He has said that we must work as well as pray. I have decided that the time has come for me to start working.*

*Fran, unless you have decided, like Paul, that you should remain in the unmarried state, will you consider whether you feel, as I do, that we could possibly learn to love each other? I appreciate that for you the issue is not quite as simple as all that, because you must also consider whether my age (43) and children would be too great an obstacle. I would be very pleased to visit with you at your convenience, or, if you prefer, send you a ticket to come here. I find talking so much easier than writing. I have not discussed with anyone that I would contact you and would like you to keep it confidential, however, feel free to discuss this with Janey if you so desire. She has been a great help to me in the past year and knows and understands me better than anyone. I am sending this letter to the school because I do not have your address at home. Awaiting your reply I remain,*

*Sincerely Yours*
*Pieter*

I have no idea how, or what, I taught that afternoon, but my students did share with me later on that they were wondering what was up with me.

I shared the letter with my Dad, and then I called big sis Grace and asked her to come over. She dropped everything and was there in a few minutes. I let her read the letter, and we talked about it together.

Dad immediately said, "Don't worry about me at all. You need to do what you want with your life, and I will build my life." This was huge because the two of us lived together, and he found purpose and joy in cooking my dinners and just having me come home each day. This would change his life dramatically, too. I was well aware of that, and my heart was breaking for him, but also thankful for his selflessness.

That weekend, I drafted my careful reply.

*Jan 22, 1982*

*Dear Pieter,*

*I received your letter today at school and, needless to say, it has given me a lot to think about. My first feelings were of surprise and, I can best describe it as excitement. I think that every girl looks forward to the day that she will be married. For me it seems that the Lord has had other plans for me up until now. He has guided and directed my life in such a way that the job He has given me has always been more of a priority in my life than anything else. I have learned to accept this quite happily because I have also learned that unless I am doing the Lord's will, I will not find peace and contentment. However, I know too that I must live life one day at a time and follow God's leading. I have often prayed about this, for I would dearly love to have someone to love. Someone with whom I can really share all the things that are important in my life. I have my family and friends who are a great help but when it comes right down to it, I still must face life's problems and joys alone. That is why your letter left me feeling quite happy. Maybe this is God's answer to my prayers.*

*On the other hand it also makes me quite nervous and afraid. I have become quite an independent person and am secure in the kind of life I now lead. I have never been a wife before, and I would have to leave familiar surroundings and roles for a very different lifestyle. I wonder if I can do it well? Peter, your age makes little difference to me. I'll be 32 in February, and I'm sure that there are many happy couples with such age differences. As for the children, I have made a career out of working with and loving children. If they are willing to accept me, then I think I could soon learn to love and care for them.*

*The most important aspect is, as you said in your letter, if we could learn to love each other. Although I don't know you well, I do think that if we go in the love of the Lord that we will be able to learn this. It's too bad that we live so far apart. Because of school responsibilities, I won't be able to come out to see you until mid-March. However, if you are able to come here, I would be glad to see you. It doesn't matter when since I'm sure I can arrange things to suit.*

*Sincerely*
*Frances Harsevoort*
*163 Old Orchard Rd*
*Burlington, Ont*
*L7T 2G2*

It didn't take long to get a reply back but those days felt long.

*Jan. 28, 1982*

*Dear Frances,*

*Thank you for your quick and positive reply to my letter. Your letter also gave me a feeling of excitement and some surprise. True, we do not know each other well, but we have met and know something about each other. My impression of you was, "an attractive and intelligent girl, how come she is unattached?" I am not so sure that every girl would look forward to being married; maybe women's lib has given me this idea. In any case it seems to me that some are confirmed spinsters, and I am glad that you do not belong to that variety. Secondly, how is your impression of me? Do I, in your mind, warrant another look? I am very happy that you too would dearly love to have someone to love and share things that are important with. You are right, it is a great help to have family and friends. I have certainly experienced this in the last year. My family, especially Janey, have been very good to me. We have an excellent housekeeper in Frieda and I have some friends that I can really talk to, but it cannot replace a good marriage relationship. This is not really surprising when you think about it for the Lord created man in His own image as male and female, all that He has created was good, and even though man has fallen, In Christ we do have already now the beginning of eternal life.*

*Yes, you are quite nervous and afraid. That I can understand very well. That I expected and we must talk about it. I hesitated writing to you for that very reason. The change for you will be much greater than for me. You will have to move away from your family and friends. We cannot start with just the two of us. Am I asking too much of you?*

*I am planning to visit you next week Friday and Saturday. If I leave Friday morning I will be approximately 5:00 p.m. in Burlington. I will phone you Monday or Tuesday and let you know.*

*Sincerely yours*
*Piet*

Over the next week or so, a few more letters and phone calls gave Piet enough confidence and encouragement to come visit me. Under the guise of a quick business trip, he arranged to fly out Friday afternoon, February 5$^{th}$, and go home again Saturday evening. Now, I needed to let a few more people in on it. Margaret and her husband, Harpert, were recruited to host Dad for the weekend. I begged the afternoon off school, so I had to give my principal a bit of the story. And so, one wintery Friday afternoon, I drove to the Toronto airport and waited anxiously as a whole line of businessmen disembarked from the Vancouver flight, hoping that I would recognize him. I played a bit of a mind game asking myself as each passenger passed by, "What if it's him?" But then the familiar face with a shy smile appeared, and I knew that this was the one I wanted.

We found a nearby restaurant to break the ice with a glass of wine and a nice dinner. Then we drove back to Burlington and continued sharing our stories.

Pieter told me of his grieving and loss, and how and when he realized that he was ready to go on again. He related how an elderly gentleman he knew and highly respected intentionally came to visit him with the message that he should get married again. He struggled with this for a while, perplexed and wondering what to do with this advice. Then, my name came into his head and wouldn't leave. So, finally, he had written the most important and challenging letter of his life. Since he didn't have my address and didn't want to raise any suspicions, he had sent it to the school he knew I taught at. He was still awestruck, never having believed that God would work in such a direct and personal manner, and yet, here he was.

Then I was able to share my story about how I had actually, though with much scepticism, been waiting for his letter. Unrelatedly, I thought at the time, I had decided in early January to not seek other positions or advancements. We were both amazed and convinced that God had led both of our paths and was now bringing them together. That provided a calm confidence and a deep joy. It wasn't until about a year later, when I was thinking back over it all, that it struck me just how enormous this decision to leave my father, family, career, and community was. And yet, we both made it with a great deal of peace. We talked, it seems, all through the night and the next day, and that afternoon, I drove him back to the airport.

I called brother Ben and Hanna from the airport and asked if I could drop in for a coffee. This was unusual, since they lived in north Toronto, too far away to just drop in. But soon, I was able to share my joy and story with them and the rest of the siblings. It would be a few more weeks before they would get to meet him, but they were all very happy and supportive.

That was Saturday. Monday evening, I sat down to write him again.

*Mon, Feb. 8, 1982*

*Dearest Piet,*

*Well, I've made it through two days without you now. I'm still way up in the clouds somewhere and the situation still seems so unreal. I've told my family and the staff at school as well as a few friends. I really enjoy watching their reactions. Most people stare in stunned disbelief at first and then are really happy for me. It must be pretty obvious to them that I'm madly in love. I just feel like standing on my head, or shouting from a rooftop, it makes me so deliciously happy. On the other hand I almost want to keep it a secret for a while so that I can savour it in all its details.*

*Piet, you've made me a pretty happy girl. I'm afraid I'm also becoming a pretty useless teacher. Your face always seems to come between me and what I'm supposed to be doing. I'll have to get myself under control again.*

*Today I was reading a chapter of a novel we are studying with the class. It's about a boy, David, who escapes from a concentration camp and makes his way to freedom. He is happy that he can enjoy freedom and independence and beauty all around him. Then he spends some time with a family and sees what love is. After he leaves, he feels that there is no purpose for remaining free, no reason to live since he can never know that love. Today I really knew what he meant.*

*Piet, I'm still amazed that everything has gone so beautifully so quickly. I would worry because it's all too good to be true except that I know that it comes from God. It's a miracle that I've waited for a long time, but it is well worth the wait. It makes me feel humble and unworthy when I see how happy it has made you.*

*Piet, I hope that you won't be disappointed in me. I hope and pray that I really will be able to give you the support and love and companionship that you need. If you are happy, then I'll be happy too. I think that you understand me well, and I'm confident that you will be good for me since I need someone I can depend on and feel secure with. I think that my needs are fairly simple, but you are a pretty complex personality. You know what you want and what you must do and you are able to do it well. I wonder if I'll be able to keep up with you and understand you? However, I also can hardly imagine being without you now.*

*I'm glad that your parents and kids are happy about it. I must admit that I'm nervous about meeting them for the first time. I'm afraid I'll be so shy I won't say a word or end up saying and doing all the wrong things. But then I worried before you came and look how well that worked out. Henk (my principal) said that I could have the Monday off, so that's no problem.*

*I'd better stop writing and get to bed now so that I can function near normal tomorrow. We're supposed to be getting more snow tonight and tomorrow so maybe we'll get another day off. I won't count on it, however, since then they never happen.*

*I hope the next two weeks fly by because I can hardly wait to be with you again. I love you, Piet.*

*Yours, in love*
*Fran*

And I wrote again on Tuesday.

*Feb. 9, 1982*

*Dear Piet,*

*It's getting late, and I should be in bed catching up on some sleep, but I wanted to write you yet. Today has been another very full, very exhausting day. It contained a lot of wonderful things, the nicest one being your phone call to start my day. Piet, when I'm with you or talking to you, then everything seems all right. I got your letter this afternoon too. It's especially wonderful when we can see that this joy is a beginning of the perfect joy in Christ. It is the security of knowing that it is God's work and God's will for us to be happy that allows me to hope for success. When we both dedicate our lives to serve and glorify God first, and when we can really share that commitment to Him, then God will bless us.*

*Another thought that has been going through my mind is the image of the church as the bride of Christ and for wives to be submissive to their husbands, for the husband is the head of the wife as Christ is head of the Church. I've had some difficulties with this concept, for I've often found it difficult to be submissive to those in authority or in a higher position—especially if I disagreed with them or had little respect for their ideas or authority. (Don't say I didn't warn you!!) However, now I think I'm beginning to understand—and I'm not even a wife yet. I don't think it would be too difficult for me to subject myself to you, for I know that you think and act the way you do because of a well thought out and heartfelt commitment to God. Piet, I really respect you and love you first of all for that.*

*I've been busy telling more people about us.*

*The other thing about today is that I got the plane tickets for next weekend. I'll be arriving on Fri Feb 19 at 8:30 pm on CP Air. I'll have to leave on Monday at 1:30 pm. I'm looking forward to seeing you and being with you, but I'm still nervous about it. Oh well, I'm sure I'll get through it.*

*That was the good part of the day. Luckily that was also most of the day. I've been feeling really tired today, and the kids at school just seemed to grow rowdier as the day went on. Actually, they were pretty good up until the last half hour when everything seemed to happen at once. I was chewing some kids out in the hallway for misbehaving when someone broke a bottle of India Ink all over the classroom floor. Of course, they all had to gather round and then those with ink on their socks tracked it all around the room and out in the hall. I was ready to quit then, I'll tell you. Anyways, I got it all cleaned up and everyone sent home on time, and soon could laugh about it too. I wasn't the only one who had problems today with the kids so that made me feel better. Teaching has its drawbacks, but it has so many rewards too. It's really nice when the kids trust you enough to tell you their problems and let you help them. And, especially there are so many opportunities to show them the joys and comforts, as well as the responsibilities of being "in Christ."*

*The other not so good part of my day was that I felt afraid again. I think it's finally starting to sink in. When I hear you talk about how happy you are and how much you love me, I feel unworthy. Do you love me, or an illusion of me? It's going to be a big task to make myself deserve your love and live up to your expectations. Piet, don't build me up too much and don't soar too high on the clouds. I'm just plain ordinary me. I can be difficult and moody and it takes me a while to fully understand where I am and where I'm going. It's important that I try to be myself with you and I will try, but it will take some time before I even know who I am and where I'm going or what I'm doing in my new role as your wife. I'm counting on you to understand and to help me find myself again for I will be lost for a while. There are so many things to learn and do and I'll feel very self-conscious about it for a while so won't do as well as I'd like. Please don't expect too much Piet. I love you and that makes it so much more important that I don't let you down. Yet, I don't think I even really know what love is in the way that you do. I have so much to learn. Please be a patient teacher for, even though I'm scared, I can't imagine life without you anymore.*

*I'd better quit now and get to bed. I really do love you!*

*Love,*
*Fran*

Meanwhile, these letters from Piet crossed paths with mine in the mail.

*Feb. 6, 1982*

*Dearest,*

*I am now still in the plane from Calgary to Vancouver. I had a snooze and feel just great. I had a little cry because I am so happy. The Lord has given me so much and I just have to let you know, or try to anyway, how I feel. The Lord had created man in righteousness and holiness, that means that he could live his life for His pleasure. He also gave man his blessing and orders, be fruitful and multiply and fill the earth and subdue it and have dominion over it. Note first be fruitful, then dominion. The essence of righteousness is to obey God's orders. That will lead into rewarding ways. That also gives great joy. Procreation is commanded and when we obey there will also be great joy in the relationship between man and wife and yes, also sex. Remember the Song of Songs. However, man fell and died, but God did not leave us in that state. He gave His promise and put enmity between us His children, and Satan. Then He gave His laws. The Psalmist says that in keeping God's law is great joy. We do not have to keep that law to the letter for Christ has fulfilled it. We are righteous again. But God did not leave it at that. He gave us His gifts, but first of all the higher gift, the more excellent way, His love. So, we can love, and I can't say it any better than Montague in his definition:*

*A succinct definition of love is that it is the ability, by demonstrative acts, to confer survival benefits on others in a creatively enlarging manner.*

*That is exactly what we are experiencing. That is what I enjoy so much to be able to bestow survival benefits and, of course, receive same from you. Sorry for the messy writing, but I am too excited to do better and, of course, the plane shakes.*

*Love*
*Piet*

*P.S. Is it not very great that His plan is being fulfilled and will come to its completeness and that he will use us?*

*P.P.S. Enclosed find my business card with the addresses and phone numbers. I am generally in Surrey from 8-10 and in Abbotsford from 12-3.*

*P.P.P.S. I forgot to tell you that you have very beautiful eyes.*

*It is real*

*Mon. Feb 15, 1982*

*Beloved*

*Received your letter this morning and here are my reactions. That sounds too business-like, but it is no use trying to hide that trait in me, for you will find out anyway if you haven't already. That most people react in stunned disbelief proves that my fears about you being a confirmed spinster were at least shared by others. On the other hand, it is not all that uncommon for a young girl to have a giant crush on an old(er) man. What is uncommon that a sedate father of 6 children can fall so far so fast. I, for one, still find it difficult to believe even though I know that it is true. I was hoping that we would learn to love each other over a period of time, but not in my wildest dreams did the possibility occur that it would happen the way it did.*

*Remember you were worried about the children accepting you, and I told you that I was not worried about that as long as we were happy? Well, Cindy and Rachel tell me at least twice a day that they are so happy. This is obviously because they notice the change in me; they are so looking forward to meeting you. Norma and Bill are also happy for me and will do their best to accept you. We cannot ask for anything more. From Phil and Mike, I cannot get much response. I guess that is to be expected at that age.*

*You are still a little worried whether I will be satisfied with you. Well Fran, I can understand that because I have the same doubts about me being able to make you happy. But I must admit that I am getting less and less worried. Please don't worry too much about it. I think that you will not have too much of a problem figuring me out, and I am really not very complex.*

*An intelligent woman like you should have me figured out in short order. And if so far you have not been totally overwhelmed by everything that I have thrown at you, you will come through with flying colours. I feel guilty for submitting you to so much at once. I was full of my experience the night before I met you, and when you kept up with me, I just let go. You have therefore seen me at my worst, it can therefore only get better.*

*Oh yes, one should write about the weather and such, well I can't say that I have noticed much of it the last 2 weeks. I'm sure we have had some but it didn't make a lasting impression. I wonder if you have anything to do with that? It seems to me that we had a lot of rain. I hope that it will be nice when you get here because otherwise you might decide not to marry me. I hope too that the days will fly by but so far there has not been much flying. O well, only four more days. We should make it.*

*Love*
*Piet*

*Tues Feb 23*

*To my dearly beloved,*

*I was just thinking how great it is to be in love with, and to be loved by you. My feelings for you have solidified considerably again. The feeling is greater, but also more solid, down to earth, if you know what I mean. I hated to see you leave but on the other hand it was easier than last time because our relationship has become more real, and I know that it will become even more so. One week and 4 days does seem like a long time but if I compare that with what I had 2 months ago, what a difference. What a blessing I have received, that you may be, and want to be my betrothed and that I may not only know it but also feel it in my heart. It is indescribable. It is wonderful that you also have the same feeling, therefore it does not matter if I can not describe it. You understand already anyway. I sure look forward to sharing the rest of my life with you. I can't think of anything I would rather do. It appears that you have passed the test as far as my family is concerned; at least my father and Joanne expressed a favourable opinion. I suppose that indicated one of two things; they make snap decisions, or they are biased. On the other hand, it could also be that they are like me, namely they recognize excellence when they see it. After all that, I better remind you of our agreement – you worry about me and I worry about everything else. Otherwise, you will be afraid again that you can't live up to all that.*

*Fran, I am in love with you, not some high ideal that I have imagined. And I also know that the Lord will give us all we need to overcome all difficulties if only we will ask Him.*

*Love Piet*

Over the next few months, we put on a lot of air miles. I flew west about once per month on WardAir or Canadian Airlines, and he came east at least once a month, so we saw each other at least every other weekend. In between, we talked on the phone daily and even wrote the occasional letters. He would set his alarm for 4:30 a.m. to call me before I left for school.

We married July 16, 1982. It was a sunny, very hot Ontario July day. Pieter and I walked down the long aisle of my home church, arm in arm. I was wearing a beautiful white gown, complete with long sleeves, a high neckline, and a stylish, wide-brimmed matching hat. The church was crowded with family, friends, students, and other well-wishers.

All the kids were involved in one way or another. Norma played the organ, Bill chauffeured us around, Phil and Mike ushered, and Cindy and Rachel were the cute flower girls. Janey was there as my witness—a bittersweet day for her. She had been such a strong support for Piet after Rika's death and was happy to see him happy again. Yet, grieving never really stops.

Pieter's parents and many of his siblings flew out for the celebration. Jack, his brother, business partner, and best friend, was there as Pieter's witness. And, thankfully, his younger brother, John, was there along with their two oldest girls. At the end of a fun dinner and party, Pieter and I left for a quiet week together. Naively, we forgot to pay for the wedding venue, so brother John came to the rescue. Thanks John! That was much appreciated.

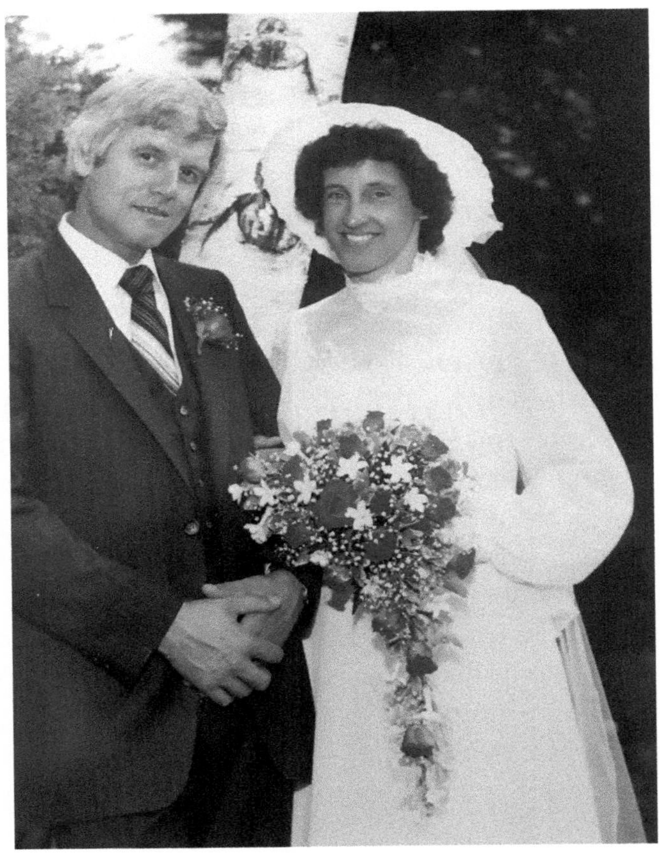

*July 16, 1982. It was a hot, humid Ontario day but we stayed cool and so enjoyed everything about the day.*

*L to R: Mike, Bill, Cindy, Me, Pieter, Rachel, Norma, and Phil.*

Norma and Bill had to fly back home for their jobs and several of my family members had offered to provide hospitality to Phil, Mike, Cindy, and Rachel for a week, so Pieter and I got one glorious week at a private cottage in beautiful Caledon Hills region of Ontario. It was lovely. Then, we gathered the kids, packed everything up, said our goodbyes to my family, and flew to Surrey to begin our new stage of life.

Dad decided to sell the house and move into Elim Villa, a small complex of seniors' apartments in Waterdown that was home to people with a similar background—Dutch immigrants from Reformed churches. He tried his best to be happy here, making new friends, and helping and supporting where he could. He also made it a regular practice to visit the sick and frail in his church on a weekly basis. Once a week, he would drop in on each of his children, bringing a stash of chocolate bars for the grandkids. These were tough years for him. He was no longer working. His time as elder in the church was in the past. And he was alone, without the love and support he had depended on his whole adult life. I called him regularly, wrote some letters, and visited him at least once a year. Pieter would visit or stay with him when he was on one of his fairly frequent business trips in the area. And he would sometimes board an airplane to come see us in Surrey. My brothers, sisters, and relatives were also very intentional about keeping him included and feeling loved and appreciated. He lived in Elim Villa for many years until his health deteriorated, and the family didn't trust him to be on his own. Herman and Jane made room for him in their home and family, and I believe these were the happiest years for him after Mom died and I moved away. Eventually, even that was not enough, and he moved into Shalom Manor, a Christian Nursing Home, where he died on May 6, 2002.

# CHAPTER 20

## Surrey BC: A New Life (July 1982)

Life looked so different now. I had moved four thousand kilometres away from my family and the community where I was well known and respected. Now, I was Pieter's wife. Mrs. Vanderpol. Changing my name hit me a lot harder than I thought it would. I was known professionally for fourteen years as Miss Harsevoort. This name also linked me to my parents, my siblings, and any past relationships and accomplishments. Now, my new name linked me to a family I still needed to get to know, that had many associations and accomplishments in this community.

I had a huge learning curve. How to be a wife? How to be a wife to a man that had been so happy with a beautiful woman, the love of his life for twenty years? Piet would often recall how he had met her at a wedding and went to great effort to get back home to pick up his own car just so that he could offer to drive her home. They were young and in love.

Together, they built a life and a family. They figured out how to parent and balance their roles together. They dreamed their dreams, and they made and carried out their plans. They built routines and family traditions together. Then, it all came to a sudden and tragic end on that highway between Houston and Smithers when a group of intoxicated young partiers suddenly made a turn right in front of them. Pieter couldn't avoid the collision.

I had to learn how to be a wife to a man who had held his first and only love in his arms and heard her say "I love you, and I love Jesus," before she died at the scene.

*Young and in love!*

*Rika and Pieter's engagement picture*

*Together they dreamed dreams and built a family.*

*Rika seated with Rachel on her lap and Cindy in front of her. Back LtoR: Norma, Bill, Pieter, Mike and Phil in the home she designed and built in Surrey.*

How do you relate to a man who spent many months pounding on heaven's doors, wondering how God could rob him of his most precious possession? Didn't God see how much he needed her? And those dear children that she had loved so much and so well? How could God let them suffer their grief and have to adjust to growing up without her? I knew all of these things because we talked of them often. Pieter would not tolerate easy answers or platitudes. He had to wrestle with it until he either found the answers or learned to submit, and even marvel at, the depths and complexity of a God so incomprehensible to our human mind. The Bible Book of Job spoke to him in very new and deep ways.

I also had to learn how to be a second wife, yet not compare myself, or be compared to another one. It was important for me to create my own unique identity and role. Pieter said once, "I'm sorry that you are getting a second-hand husband, one who comes in a package with six kids." But I never saw it that way. "No," I responded, "I'm getting an experienced husband. And your kids are precious gifts."

Rika had taken a young naïve heart and carefully tended and nurtured it into a mature husband. Rika had been the one to teach him that her needs were important too. She had taught him how to love her and their children while running the business. She made my life richer that way. But how would I ever be able to be a good wife to a strong-willed and determined man, eleven and a half years older, and so much more experienced in everything our new life held? I learned from him how to take care of the household, partly because I didn't want to make a lot of change to their daily life, and partly because so much of it was new to me.

Yes, I knew I was a second wife, but I also always knew that Pieter did not ever compare me to her or expect me to be like her. He has always cherished what Rika was in his life. But he had also learned that you cannot love a memory. Life goes on, and we must live in the present. God had made it so clear to both of us, in distant parts of the country and unknown to the other, that God had a vision for us to be together. Pieter has always encouraged me to be myself and do things my way.

After all the change that had happened that summer—moving four thousand kilometres away from my family and familiar world, retiring from my career as a teacher, leaving everything but my clothes and personal possessions behind—I wasn't too sure about who I was.

I also had to learn how to be a mom to kids who were still hurting and lost in the grief of missing their Mom. We didn't know how to deal with grief very well. We still don't, but we at least acknowledge it better. I had taught children for fourteen years, but I didn't feel like it helped me parent better. Actually, trying to parent these lovely children, seeing how vulnerable they are when they are outside of the structures of the classroom, made me realize I would probably have been a better teacher if I had been a parent first.

I had to learn to be a daughter-in-law and sister-in-law in an established family that had its complex relationships and the complications of a successful family business.

And I had to learn the simpler, but nonetheless overwhelming, lessons about keeping a household organized, nourished, clean, and happy. How and what do I cook for a family that had been spoiled by a Mom, and later a housekeeper, that knew their likes and dislikes and were excellent cooks and homemakers? Frieda, the housekeeper, left me a list of meal ideas with detailed instructions, which was helpful. She had learned by going to the recipes on the 'smudgiest' pages of the cookbooks to find the favourites. I learned the routines such as, "chicken on Thursdays so you could have leftovers for the rice casserole for Sunday." And a fancy dessert every night? Apple or butterscotch pie? Cream Puffs? Strawberry shortcake? I spent half my day despairing over making desserts! Baking became part of my routine—bread, squares, and cookies for daily snacks, and then the Christmas baking! Almond-filled speculaas, puff pastries, Dutch letter cookies… I was so out of my league.

Then, there were the endless loads of laundry to be sorted, knowing which socks belonged to whom (they all had a colour-coded thread on the toe to help). Four-year-old Rachel was a fountain of knowledge and help with these details. Mending and darning socks (I kept it up for a while, and then I gave up in despair). There were also stories to read, toys to be kept in some semblance, swimming lessons, doctor's appointments, lunches to make, bread to bake, cookies to be ready for after-school teatime, and the ever-present garden needing something picked and processed every day of the summer.

I set my priorities. First of all, make as few changes as you can get away with. Defer to Dad, always—he knows them best. Use the same recipes. Don't rearrange the furniture. Keep the routines, and keep up family relationships.

My time was spent in the home getting to know my husband and our children. Pieter was a great support—he was very patient and encouraging. And the kids tried their best too.

For Cindy and Rachel, having a Mom again was important. They were four and eight when we married, and unfortunately, had few rational memories of their Mom. We knew so little about grief and trauma and its effects back then. Rachel was home with me for the first year. A very observant child, she was a great help with details, and it was lots of fun seeing life through her eyes. Rachel was a happy child, eager to learn and keep up with her older sister. She could keep us all entertained with her comments. She knew exactly what she wanted, and she really liked her routines. Toast with Cheez Whiz melted in the microwave was her favourite lunch for a long time.

Cindy happily went off to second grade. She was quieter and very sweet. She would come home and tell me all she had learned at school over the customary cup of tea. Cindy and Pieter had developed an especially close bond because they shared a love for reading. Rika had always read stories to the kids, so Pieter had taken that over. However, he wasn't interested in reading the typical small children's picture books, so he chose to read books like the Chronicles of Narnia to Cindy. She lapped it all up, tucked snugly beside him in his chair. Her bedtime was often extended because they needed to read just one more chapter.

Mike and Phil were teenage boys, both in high school. They were twelve and fourteen—that awkward age when mothers, at the best of times, have challenges relating to their sons. And being new to the family and community, I didn't have insights and connections into their past, schools, and friends. Each in their own way, they tried their best to make it all work, and I appreciated it very much.

Mike was an introverted putterer. He loved to take things apart to see how they worked. His bedroom was constantly cluttered with so many small parts of this and that. And he loved to read. Mike never had much to say, and it took me a while—far too long, and even then, I didn't learn it well enough—to learn that when Mike walked past me and said a few words, I needed to pay attention. He won't elaborate or repeat himself, so listen well and take note. In his quiet way, he would notice when I was struggling with something and would just step in and help. I remember awkwardly trying to iron when he noticed that the setup was for a left-handed person, which Rika had been, and quickly readjusted to make it easier for right-handed me to do. Other times, he would come and wordlessly scoop up a crying baby so I could focus on making dinner.

Phil was more talkative and ready to share what was happening in his life or his thoughts. He had an after-school job unloading trucks at Vanderpol's Eggs, together with his cousin Kelly, so between school, unloading trucks, and other chores, Phil was pretty busy. Phil also showed his leadership abilities in organizing the daily after-dinner kitchen cleanup. I'm not sure the younger siblings always appreciated it, but the kitchen would be spotless when they were done.

Phil and Mike, along with their cousin Kelly, who lived at the other end of the lane, were partners in BEVA Dairy.

BEVA Dairy, a combination of *Be*rends and *Va*nderpol, had been started a number of years earlier by our oldest son, Bill and some of his cousins down the lane, the Berends family. Pieter mentored them on the business aspects, and,I'm sure Opa Vanderpol helped keep an eye on the cows. Now, a few years later, the Berends family had moved away, and Jack and Marna had moved onto the business property. Bill was away at college, so it fell to Phil, Mike, and Kelly to keep the business going. They took turns caring for and milking three or four cows in our small barn every morning and evening. This provided delicious fresh milk and cream for our family, as well as much of the extended family and a few friends.

Bill had graduated from high school and was away working on his uncle's farm in Coaldale Alberta, then studying agriculture at Olds College. I didn't really get to know him until a bit later. He came home for Christmas holidays, but he spent his summers away working on farms. I mostly got to know him through long telephone conversations on Sunday evenings. But that wasn't until later.

Norma was studying music at UBC. She was the one who struggled the most with our marriage, deeply hurt in seeing her father in love again, seemingly having forgotten his first love. Also, she had played an important role in the family for the past year and a half, and now the little girls were coming more and more to me for care and affection, and her father was content spending his evenings sharing his stories and thoughts with me. Now, she could go back to being a bit more carefree, but it just wasn't the same. I didn't know how to reach her very well, but I tried my best to let her know that I could not, and never wanted to, replace her mother. But I did want to be a friend and support for her.

While I had met Rika a few times, I can't say that I knew her well. I wanted to keep her reality alive in the home but didn't know how. Her picture was always prominent on the family room wall, and her things, as close as possible to the way they had been. There were many times when I would sit staring at her picture, wishing with all my heart that she could come and reach out to this or that struggling child, or teach me how to mother them. I really felt, and continue to feel, accountable to her. I was called to continue her task and responsibility toward her children and husband. She would have loved to be able to finish those tasks. I also felt her presence and support.

I tried to build relationships with Rika's parents and siblings, the VanDyk clan, in the hope that they would share stories about Rika with her kids. Since they were caught up in the awkwardness and pain of grief, that didn't work as well as I had hoped. Yet, we did build relationships. Janey and I remained good friends. She was very supportive in many ways, but especially in helping me understand and navigate the family dynamics in what became my third family—another set of in-laws. We continued to celebrate, and even host the VanDyk Christmas until it got too big for one house. We visited back and forth and journeyed to Smithers or Coaldale, Alberta, in the summers to keep those ties strong and build on old memories. Some family reunions helped keep connections stronger. And, over time, I enjoyed a very good relationship with Oma VanDyk, even calling her Mom.

Pieter and I thought it made good sense to put off having more children until I had built good relationships with the ones we had. However, soon after we were married, I longed to experience motherhood with my body too, thinking that I might be a better parent if I went through all the physical and hormonal changes of pregnancy. So, talking it over together, we listened to my instincts and stopped the birth control. Soon after, I became pregnant. I'm not sure how I managed being pregnant with all the other demands and stresses, but I did, and in May, ten months after our marriage, our daughter Elsa was born.

A home with a newborn baby is a magical place. Both birth and death usher us into a sacred space of awe, love, and gentleness. Heaven's doors have opened to release or receive a soul back again. And we are all touched by the holiness.

Elsa was their sister. Elsa was my daughter. We were now intimately connected as a family with this tiny, snuggly, seven-pound-and-eight-ounce infant. We named her Elsina Hendrika, after my mother, Siena, and Pieter's first wife, whose full name, Hendrika Lena, had been shortened to Rika. Three families now joined together in one, symbolized and embodied in a tiny bundle of new life.

*My Dad came spending precious moments with Elsa.*

*Elsa at one yr.*

*Mike has a magic touch with babies and children.*

*Our home in Surrey*

Over the next twelve years, we welcomed five more children. Margaret Hanna, named after my youngest sister, Margaret, and my sister-in-law, Hanna; Joanna Grace (Joni), named after Pieter's oldest sister, Joanne, and my oldest sister, Grace; Benjamin Joel, named after my Dad, Calvin David (King David and John Calvin; and John Herman, named after most of the rest of the family. All of the children continued to grow and mature, each in their own time and their own way.

While an onlooker might have seen chaos, confusion, and children maybe not getting the one-on-one they needed and deserved, I saw teenage boys coming home to be greeted enthusiastically by a grinning, excited toddler, wanting hugs and play. Babies were passed from shoulder to shoulder to be rocked to sleep. There was usually someone around to talk to, play with, take out your frustrations on, or whatever else. Besides our own house full of kids, it was a place where friends were always welcome, whether it was pulling up another chair to the dinner table or offering a bed to sleep in when you needed an escape.

It sounds like an idyllic version of the reality, and it is. There were many frustrations, unmet needs and expectations, gaps, and misunderstandings. Around the time I turned sixty, there was a period when the rush had settled a bit, and I had time to think. I groaned out my confessions and repentance before God. *How could I have …? Or not have…? Why didn't I realize …? How could I have been so stupid?* I was entrusted, by God and by Rika, to personalize the love and wisdom of God for these children, and I did it so poorly. Why didn't I know more about grieving and take more concrete steps to address it? The Bible says that in the last days, the book of judgment will be opened. The book of my life lay open before me, and I squirmed. And I wept. And I repented.

And then I realized that it wasn't about me. My weakness was carried in God's strength, which is love. I didn't need to be the perfect Mom, or the perfect wife, or the perfect anything. I needed to go back to twenty-one-year-old me, learning to walk hand in hand with God in a messy world, just loving our neighbour, and our family, the best we can with what we have.

# CHAPTER 21

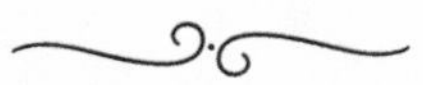

## My In-Laws: Next Door Neighbours

*Dad, Opa, Willem Vanderpol*

*Mom, Oma, Stijntje Vanderpol*

The summer after we were married, Pieter's parents, who I also now called Mom and Dad, sold their hobby farm and built a house next door to us. Every day, Dad would poke his head into our doorway to deliver the Vancouver Sun. We shared a subscription, which he would read early in the morning and then bring our way. It was a combination of environmental awareness and frugality. If I wasn't too busy, I'd invite him in for a chat, which he and I both really enjoyed. We got along well, and I learned a lot from him, especially about my husband.

Then, he'd walk down the lane to visit Pieter and Jack in the office to catch up on business matters. Usually, the men's conversation eventually went to the Sunday sermon or the Men's Bible Study discussion. Mom would often drop in later in the afternoon to share a cup of tea. It was always cozy and homey, or as we would have said it in Dutch, *gezellig*.

Dad really wanted a dog. Mom didn't. It made him sad. Well, I hated to see him sad, so I suggested that he find the dog he wanted, and we would get it. He could walk it every day and spend as much time with it as he wanted. I thought this would be a nice compromise to make everyone happy. So, he found a beautiful German Shepherd, Shadow, and we were happy to have her. Mom soon had a change of heart, however, and Shadow became their dog full-time.

Then, Dad started to show signs of Alzheimer's. These were such hard years for him and Mom. Dad voluntarily gave up his driver's licence when he realized that he could no longer trust himself. We watched with sadness as he became more confused and disoriented. Yet, the kids were so caring and helpful, and they unobtrusively and lovingly helped him with simple tasks like cutting his meat at dinner time or discretely helping him find his way back home if he was looking confused on the laneway. He taught us all so much about dealing with adversity.

One rainy autumn afternoon, he came trudging in, all upset, hunched over, with tears rolling down his cheeks. "I've lost half my brain, and I'm losing the rest quickly. And I'll be just a burden." And he wept. And I wept. I tried my best to comfort him with platitudes. And then, he suddenly stood up tall, straightened his shoulders, and said, "God has blessed me and taken care of me all my life! Now He has given me a hard thing, and I dare to complain?" Cheeks still wet with tears, but now tall and straight, he turned and walked back home. I was dumbstruck. What a legacy!

Dad wanted more than anything to be able to stay living at home with his family; we promised to keep him home as long as we could. We hired 'round-the-clock caregivers, and the family took turns visiting often. He was very loved by everyone. But, at some point, it became time to find a nursing home. Dad would sometimes wander away or become frustrated and angry. Mom found it very stressful, and she was dealing with her own health issues. She was waiting for a hip replacement and was also on heart medications.

So, Mom and I started to visit care homes. That was a very discouraging task, and we couldn't find one that we felt comfortable with. Even the best ones looked and felt like institutions rather than a home. Then, we heard of a new facility, Wintrestle, that was opening in our neighbourhood. It was a very small home with ten beds. The owners, Catherine and Andy, were the main caregivers and lived on site. They were willing to consider taking one Alzheimer's resident but wanted to meet him first to be able to assess his care levels.

I made an appointment to bring him for tea one afternoon. I went to Dad's place early to pick him up. While he was still napping in his chair I chatted with his caregiver. He soon joined in the conversation and was in one of his lucid moments, so I explained that I wanted to take him to visit and evaluate this home. He listened carefully, and then a lonely tear rolled down his cheek. "I really want to stay here," he said. "I'm afraid that if I go in a home, you will all forget me."

I said, "Dad, I promise you that we will not forget you. Every day, at least one of us will come to visit you and see that you are happy."

He came along and had a wonderful time. Catherine and Andy were very loving and hospitable, and he felt it. The next day, he went so far as to say that if you had to be in a home, that was the place to be. Catherine then asked if we could bring him for an overnight stay so they could better evaluate his care needs; so, the following Saturday evening, I dropped him off. I felt like I was leaving my child at boarding school.

We were planning to pick him up Sunday morning to take him along to church, for he still loved that. But Catherine called in the morning to say that he was not feeling up to it. She asked if we could come in the afternoon. He still didn't want to come then, so I arranged to pick him up Monday morning.

He never did come home again and lived quite happily in Wintrestle for about a year, until his death. We kept our promise to visit. Every day at least one child, and often many of the grandchildren, would be there to enjoy his company and show their love. On his birthday, June 6, 1988, a small crowd was there to share his cake. He was quite "with it," recognizing them and enjoying the festivities. After they left, he fell asleep and never woke up again. He died peacefully the following morning.

Not too long after Dad moved into Wintrestle, Mom decided that living alone was not happiness for her, so she moved into Manoah Manor, the independent-living home for our church seniors. She really enjoyed the fellowship of being among friends there, playing seemingly endless rounds of Rummikub or helping to organize the special events and activities. We continued to visit her regularly and took turns bringing her to our homes, especially for Sunday dinners.

Dad died in 1988, and Mom died five years later, in 1993. Their physical presence was forever gone, and we were now the oldest generation—no longer the children, but the ones who had to step up to the plate in carrying on the family identity. Their love, values, and faith had shaped it. We now had to work with it, adapt it to our times, and, eventually, pass on the torch to our own children.

# CHAPTER 22

## Business

I have talked a lot about the people and events that made up my life, but now I should also explain a bit about the business. Pieter was the President of Vanderpol's Eggs Ltd., a company his father founded in 1952. Pieter had left school at age fifteen to help him build it up. They started out selling fish, and soon eggs, door to door in Vancouver neighbourhoods. The business grew into a grading operation, supplying grocery stores, restaurants, and bakeries with shell eggs. They had also begun, on a very small scale, to break eggs out of their shells into pails to better serve the needs of the hospitality and food manufacturing industries in southern British Columbia. This business served a need for these markets, but just as importantly, it also provided jobs and community for many, especially from our Dutch immigrant community.

When I married Pieter, he owned it in a fifty-fifty partnership with his brother, Jack. Pieter published a book called *First with the Finest,* which tells the story of the Vanderpol family and the growth and development of Vanderpol's Eggs Ltd. This business was built by faith, trust, and hard work, building on the values and truths that Pieter's parents lived. It is also a journey of learning by doing, taking risks, making mistakes, and trusting others. It's a story of relationships within a family and church community, with employees, customers, and suppliers.

We lived on a one-acre property that had been carved out at the back of the ten-acre plot the business operated from. Jack, Marna, and their five children lived in the original house right beside the business. Piet's Mom and Dad lived next door to us. So, as you can probably understand, the business played a big part in our lives. This was another learning curve for me, as I tried to understand and support my husband as a business leader. I got to know many of the employees and tried to wrap my head around the responsibilities and culture of business ownership.

*The Mt. Lehman building. It has gone through many expansions over the years.*

Vanderpol's Eggs had expanded in 1978 by purchasing an egg further processing operation in Abbotsford. Here, the eggs that were not sold as fresh shell eggs were broken in a machine through a more dedicated process. Some of them were separated into whites and yolks, while most were mixed in huge tanks as liquid whole eggs. These products were pasteurized, lab tested, and sold as convenient fresh or frozen egg and egg products to restaurants, bakeries and food manufacturers. When there was a surplus of eggs, some of it was dried in huge, noisy dryers to be sold as powder for larger manufacturing companies.

By the early eighties, they were busy developing new products, tailored to customer needs and selling to markets across much of Canada. The business kept growing, and along with it, Pieter and his team were excitedly expanding their knowledge and vision.

This led to the next step. What started with selling eggs in the shell then led to breaking the shell open to become more familiar with, and make greater use of, the parts. This seemed to logically lead to the next step. They began developing a process to remove lysozyme from egg whites for a more specialized product that opened global markets. To deal with the increased production, we opened a plant in St Mary's, Ontario, in 1984. We did a bit of fantasizing about whether we should move to Ontario to be nearer to my family and be on a more equal footing as both newcomers to the community. However, uprooting the family was too big of a cost, so it remained a pleasant dream.

The business continued to grow and develop over the years, but I was mostly an observer and supporter. Living close to the business, I got to know many of the employees on walks down the lane or at company events. Also, many were members of the church community. Pieter really liked it when I would break away to accompany him to the annual business conference, so I met some of the national industry players as well. These conferences were held in different provinces each year, so it often allowed for a quick weekend visit to my family in Ontario on our way to the conference.

Since many of the employees were also members of our church community, it was harder to find my place in the church. In the eyes of many, I was the boss's wife, to be treated with respect but never to be one of their good friends. This was hard and lonely. I longed for my old, comfortable friendships and a sister or brother closer by. But life was full with my family, people were friendly, and life was good.

The business has been a big part of my, and our, story. Leadership and responsibility force us to become more independent thinkers with a broader outlook on life and the world. Since both Pieter and I have a strong theological basis and bent, we always struggle to ask the big questions. We had experienced God working in what seemed like unconventional ways when we found one another. We were still under the influence of and committed to that same God. So, when opportunities and possibilities presented themselves in business, we were willing and able to proceed, one step at a time.

# CHAPTER 23

## Broken Relationships in the Extended Family: Divorce

Pieter's Dad had grown up in a broken home. His father had abandoned them, his mom, and three siblings, when Dad was five. This resulted in Pieter's Dad and his siblings growing up in extreme poverty, compounded by the social stigma of abandonment, and without the provision, protection, and leadership that was a father's duty. They made it and, Dad learned to be a strong, self-reliant, and responsible leader from a very young age. Because of this pain, Dad worked very hard at building a good secure marriage for him, his wife, and their children. He believed very strongly that divorce is not ever an option. Each of us was very aware of that in the words, and example, and bar that Mom and Dad set in their own healthy marriage. And Mom and Dad took comfort, and maybe a bit of pride, in seeing each of their eight children married with families and all part of the church.

And then, Pieter's brother, Jack, and his wife, Marna, separated and divorced. This, of course, had a longer history of an unhappy marriage and a final desperate way to resolve it. Shock waves reverberated through the family. It was no surprise to anyone that the marriage was not a very healthy one, but, as no one had known how to deal with that, none of us now had any idea how to deal with divorce. We all worked hard to try to fix the marriage—we provided much support and encouragement, counsellors were brought in, and we tried anything to duct tape it back together again. But it was not to be. Divorce happened, and we had no tools, teachings, or words to deal with the failure and brokenness. Our theology taught us that we are all totally depraved and incapable of any good. Every Sunday, we were reminded that we live and are loved by God's grace alone. Yet, we didn't know how to deal with the realities of sin and brokenness, of forgiveness and grace.

Dad already was dealing with Alzheimer's at the time, so he didn't engage too much in the discussions, other than to advise Pieter not to "reward the culprit."

So, we did what we knew. When we couldn't solve "the problem," we isolated it and cut it out of our conscious lives. We allowed relationships to rupture by not accepting the realities of brokenness. We no longer had respect and acceptance for one another (on both sides), so Pieter and Jack—brothers, friends, and business partners for over thirty years—severed all of those ties. There was so much pain all around.

Then, a few years later, Theo, Pieter's youngest sibling, also divorced his wife, Nancy. Nancy was from my hometown and community of Burlington. We had been part of the same social groups as teens, and I knew her family. So, I tried my best to be like a sister to her, supporting her as well as I could during, and after, the divorce. It was the same routine. Circle the wagons to try to "fix" it. Talk, pray, support, and love. And then, when it doesn't work and the marriage is irreparably broken, we go our separate ways, leaving them to feel the effects of having failed.

Thankfully, over twenty years later, we did reconnect with both Jack and his new wife, Judy, and Theo and his new wife, Jitka, and we built relationship again. According to the old Dutch saying, "too late smart!" We have learned a bit more about brokenness and grace. We still have a long way to go, but now we can begin with saying "I love you as you are," and squeeze through the judgmental thoughts to hold them in our embrace.

# CHAPTER 24

## Death Leaves Its Painful Mark

This chapter spans a few decades of time. I have written about the grief of my Mother's death. Similarly, Pieter's wife Rika's sudden death on that highway between Houston and Smithers changed his life and those of his children forever. Our parents have passed the torch to our generation after a reasonably full life and that is painful but also 'normal'. Death continues to be a part of life.

*Sidney John Vanderwoude Aug 14, 1964 – May 5, 1984*

In 1984, my oldest nephew, Sid, died at the age of nineteen. Sid loved being with family. Family gatherings were special to him and with him and he often dropped in at relatives for a chat and some 'gezelligheid'. He was a musician, an awesome pianist and organist, just beginning to learn how to build and repair pipe organs. Now he was gone. In a moment, a car accident, his earthly sojourn was all over. The grief was just beginning. For Grace, her husband, John, and their nine other children, it was the beginning of a long, painful journey. One year later, on what would have been Sid's twenty-first birthday, his youngest sister Diane was born. Though they never met, Sid has always had a profound impact on her.

Sid Vanderwoude amid swell division pipes

*Justin Harry Vanderwoude June 27, 1973 – March 13, 1994*

Ten years later, in 1994, the unimaginable happened again when Sid's younger brother Justin died. He was twenty, and he also died in a car accident. Justin was just beginning to 'find himself' as a young adult, studying at Mohawk College and building a relationship with a girl who had connected with his heart. Grace and John were in Australia at the time to be a part of their son Jay's wedding. I can't imagine the long flight home.

*Jason Gregory Vanderwoude Feb 7, 1969 – March 15, 2014*

Twenty years later, in 2014, Jay died of lung cancer. I had taught Jay back in grade five. He had been the heart of his family for his wife Wilma and their five children and an important partner with his brothers in their business, Vanderwoude Sod. This loss was a more prolonged grief as they walked the slow and painful journey of cancer closely together with him. By this time, his sister Tasha was a very competent nurse and Diane had grown up and followed her heart to become a funeral director. Having been born in a family so affected by grief, she wanted to help other families walk that journey. She has been such a blessing for our family as she served and supported us, and she continues to help us get a better understanding of grief.

Three beautiful and precious young men that my sister bore, loved, and had dreams for now live in our hearts and memories.

*Randal Steven deLeeuw Jan 11, 1982 – May 15, 2003*

Pieter's sister, Janet, and her husband, Hans, lost their youngest son, Randy, in May 2003, also at the age of twenty, in a farm accident. He was partnering with his father on the family farm, with the potential of taking it over. Randy always seemed to have a smile on his face and was happy to take his younger cousins out for adventures on the farm. A gentle giant. Again, a young man with so much to live for whose life ended in a moment. So, life changed in so many ways for these dearly loved people.

*Bernard John Harsevoort Sept. 27, 1975 – Nov. 20, 2003*

My brother, John, and his wife, Janet, lost their oldest son, Bernie, in a workplace accident in November of that same year. After all the health issues this family had already gone through, this was such a cruel blow. Bernie's enthusiasm for life and his loving nature are so missed. He always had a smile on his face, a joke or a laugh and his genuine love and care for people shone out consistently.

These were two more families broken by grief and slowly put back together again with all of the cracks filled in with gold.

*Ruth Anita Vanderpol March 3, 1982 – Dec. 19, 1992*

Little Ruth, Bill (Pieter's brother) and Jo's youngest daughter, had been born just after Pieter and I got to know each other. As she grew, it became increasingly obvious that she had multiple challenges, physically and mentally. Ruth enriched their family for twelve years, filling their household with love and music before her tiny body gave up the struggle.

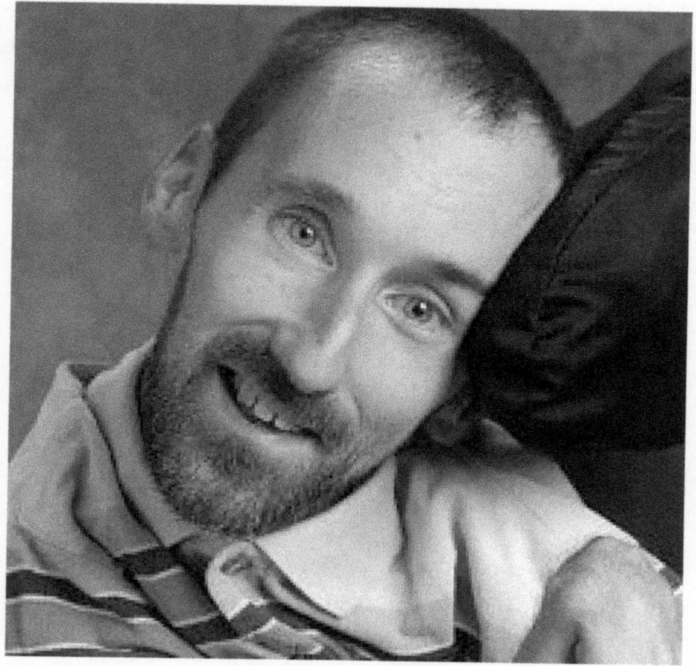

*Pieter Arend Harsevoort June 15, 1983 – Jan. 26, 2016*

Finally, Pieter, brother Herman and Jane's youngest son, had been diagnosed with spinal muscular atrophy around his first birthday. The doctor did not expect him to reach kindergarten age, but he did. Then, he graduated from elementary school, secondary school, and university, first with a bachelor's and later a master's degree. The fact that he was chosen to be the Valedictorian for his High School and Class Speaker for his University graduation is evidence of the great respect everyone had for him. He taught school for a number of years. At age thirty-four, he died, leaving a rich legacy of patience, unconditional love, acceptance, and a joy for living a full life.

Each of these people was so loved and loving. They were very precious to their parents and siblings, aunts, and uncles. Each of their deaths left painful, gaping wounds. Each of them is still a part of our story. Their lives enriched and inspired the many who loved them so much. Their deaths have hurt and wounded. All the "whys" still hang in the air.

*Tina Harsevoort (Catherina vanMiddelkoop) June 20, 1948 – Nov. 23, 2007*

My brother Harry's wife, Tina, died from a brain tumour in 2007. I was her maid of honour at their wedding. Tina loved kids – her family especially, but she also had a huge heart for foster babies. I was so touched, but not at all surprised, at how well Harry loved and cared for her during these hard times.

*Janet Harsevoort (Jannette Guesebroek) Oct 17, 1952 – Feb. 3, 2012*

My brother Little John's wife, Janet, finally got to go and be with Jesus in 2012, after going through a heart transplant and a kidney transplant. Janet's strong faith, resiliency and wisdom have left their mark on my life. I remember her face with her beautiful smile, but I also recall so many other emotions. Janet lived fully. Her physical heart grew ever weaker and more damaged but her emotional heart grew so much stronger and healthier.

HEALTH

**'Every day is a gift' to mother pulled back from brink**

By ED ROGERS
The Spectator
FLAMBOROUGH

Janet Harsevoort's story is one of faith before adversity, of religious conviction in the face of worldly despair.

The 42-year-old has been at death's door many times. She's found peace by rising above the ills of the body.

Now she is effusive in her thanks — to her four boys, her husband, her family, her neighbors and the Canadian Reformed Church congregation that supported her through six months of torment.

"I was not supposed to be here," she said. "Every day is a gift to me. I thank God for that."

In June 1993, 16 years after discovering that her heart was defective, she got an early morning call to receive a transplant. Three days later, the right side of the heart failed. The heart rebounded but soon after, she contracted a lung virus.

"It wasn't until early October that we realized that maybe she was going to live," says her husband, John.

She was unconscious most of the summer, on the brink of death. Her internal organs collapsed and machines kept her alive. Eventually, Mrs. Harsevoort's health improved and she made it home for Christmas last year.

But her kidneys never recovered. She receives dialysis three times a week and needs a kidney transplant.

In a breathy voice, she says it was a blessing to meet dedicated hospital staff as well as other transplant recipients. Her energy and strength have increased so much, she says with a smile, that the urge her boys feel to help around the house is diminishing.

Her health problems seem to have cleared a path to peace of mind. Her husband has shared the journey.

The self-employed contractor was constantly at his wife's side, shedding tears, worrying. But the overwhelming feeling was acceptance, he said.

"If she lives, it's going to be good. If she dies, it's going to be good. If you trust God, you get peace," he remembers deciding.

Meanwhile, preparing for the possibility of their mother's death has exposed the children — Bernie, 19, Len, 17 on Wednesday, Jeff, 14, and Andrew, 11 — to lessons of life others may never see, Mr. Harsevoort said.

"It was not easy to do. It was not hard either. It was a learning experience, an enriching experience.

"I'm proud of them."

Janet Harsevoort: heart transplant

My brothers have modelled love so well. I am thankful that, after a time of grieving and adjusting, they both found new partners to be happy with. So, now I have two additional sisters in Greta and Joy. Both of these women went through their own times of sorrow, and they are building new relationships on the rich soil of having to wrestle with life's big questions.

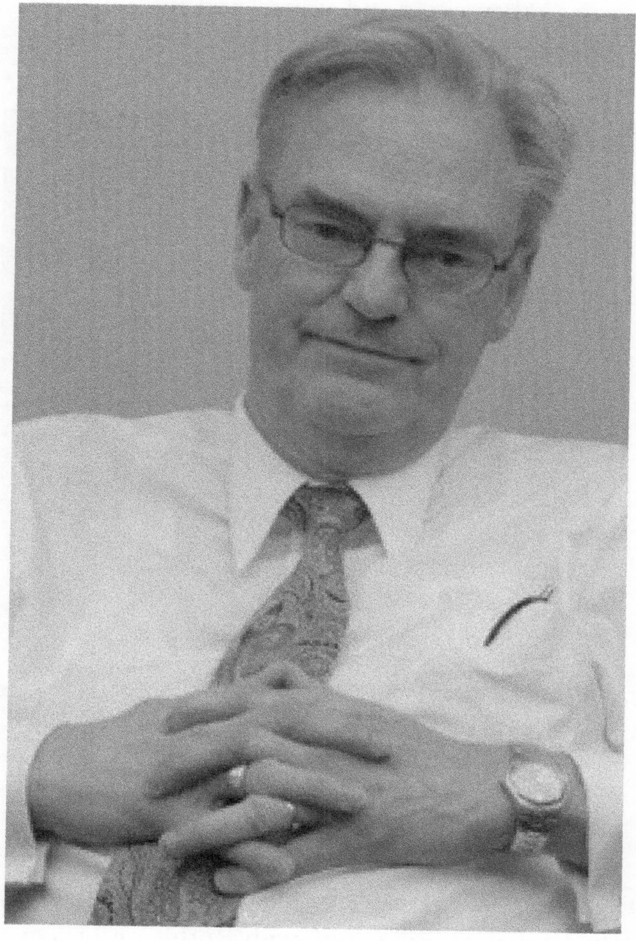

*Hendrik Aaldert Berends Jan 26, 1942 – Oct 30, 2017*

Piet's sister, Joanne, lost her husband, Henk Berends, in 2017. He was a well-respected family, business, and church leader that made for an interesting life for him and Joanne. Henk was outgoing and a good listener. I remember after I had a miscarriage they came and visited and his empathy helped me so much in helping me heal.

*Willem (Bill) Vanderpol Oct 26, 1944 – Jan. 15, 2021*

In January 2021, Pieter's brother, Bill, died suddenly from COVID-19. I recall Bill sitting with Ruthie on his lap singing to her in his deep voice. Bill had numerous serious health issues that slowed him down considerably for his last twenty-five years. He always did the hard work of recovery and rebuilding and he always maintained his faith in God and his love and respect for 'his Jo'.

*John Hutten Oct. 13, 1933 – March 24, 2021*

My Uncle John died in March after dementia robbed him of his memory. Uncle John lived a very full life. He had great difficulty sitting still – always needed to be on the move and active. I remember visiting him once just after he had been trapped by a heavy security fence, all alone. He eventually managed to squirm out from underneath, dragged himself to his truck and drove home. He was very badly bruised and in great pain. In the middle of the night the pain got so bad that he called an ambulance but insisted on making his own way down to the lobby to not inconvenience his neighbours and the ambulance attendants.

*Jacob Vanderpol Dec. 3, 1939 – May 5, 2021*

Pieter's brother, Jack, died in May after a number of years of failing health. Jack was a people person that loved sports, especially hockey and sailing. He had been Pieter's closest in age brother, best friend, and business partner until divorce got in the way and caused a painful rift for way too many years. We were all so thankful that we reconnected and re-established relationship during the later years.

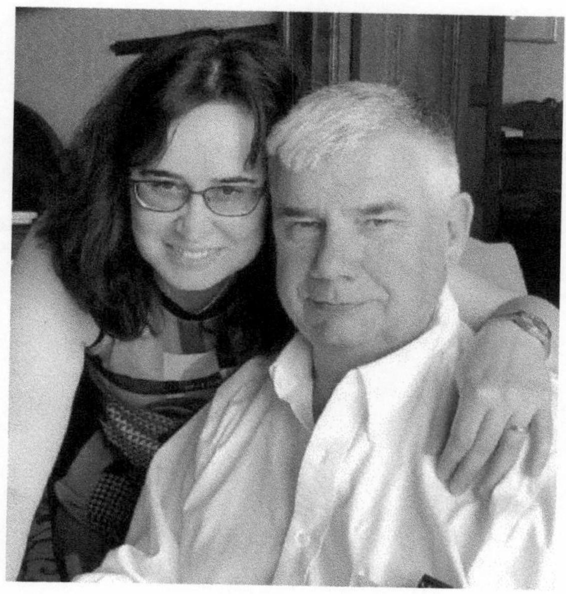

*Theodore Vanderpol*

*Jan. 11, 1951 – Dec 21, 2021*

*When I asked Jitka for a photo of Theo she replied "I don't have any photos of Theo without me, we were one body literally.."*

One more death to add to the sadness. In December of 2021 Pieter's youngest brother Theo died of cancer. Theo had moved to Prague where he met and married Jitka. They each had a child they were raising alone when they decided that it would be happiness for all of them to become one family. Jitka is a medical doctor, a neurologist and found work in northern England. Theo developed his own business there and they lived happily together raising their children. I'm so glad that Pieter and I visited with them a number of years back to restore relationships, reconnect with the old Theo and get to know Jitka and their children.

Pieter lost three brothers in one year. We are all growing older and have various health challenges, so the list of those whose earthly journey is complete will grow longer.

Bit by painful bit, we are learning to live with grief. It becomes a part of the fabric of who we are. We don't get over grief. We weave it into our lives and our reality with all its questions and emotions.

# ABBOTSFORD

# CHAPTER 25

## Moving to a New City (1990)

Pieter was dividing his time between our Surrey and Abbotsford businesses. Every day, he would make the half hour journey between the two. After Jack's divorce, when the two could no longer work as partners, they worked out a separation agreement. One of the terms was that Jack would now own the business property in Surrey. Since the area was all being developed into residential subdivisions, Jack made plans to sell. Thirty-four years after Dad had moved the business and family to this spot, in what had been rural Surrey, the business was really non-conforming to the neighbourhood. We couldn't do much to improve or expand here anymore, so the time was right to move all the operations to Abbotsford. We expanded the building to accommodate the grading operations, increased administration, and we enjoyed having all the business under one roof.

We had over twenty acres of undeveloped land there, so we chose a hilltop with a view to build a new home. We wanted something that could better suit the needs of a family that was growing in number, but also in diversity of ages and stages. We had always valued the convenience of living near the business, as it allowed the children to be more a part of it all. It was also important to Pieter that I got to design and build a new place. Rika had designed our Surrey home, and it always had her stamp on it. Now, eight years later, it was okay to move on. It was very special that we could sell the Surrey home to Rika's sister, Janey, and her husband. It held emotional memories for them as well, and it allowed for a nice transition.

I sketched out a floor plan that would suit our unique family and take advantage of the magnificent views of the north shore mountains. My little brother, John, who was by now a designer and builder of some repute back in Ontario, drew up the plans.

By this time, Norma was married to Mike Kobald, and Bill was living in Ontario, but that still left eight children, from infants to adults, to accommodate comfortably. We began laying the foundation one summer with the plan to let it settle before building the rest the following spring. I had planned for five bedrooms on the main floor of a sprawling bungalow and two downstairs in a walkout basement, for a total of seven. Soon, I knew that I had to call my brother to find a way to fit in another bedroom, because a new baby would be joining us. John fit in a cute little attic bedroom, so that problem was solved.

On July 31, 1990, four weeks before Cal was born, we moved into an unfinished house. The first night, we didn't even have electricity. The girls slept in the vacation trailer tucked behind a hill behind the house. Pieter, the little ones (Joni and Ben), and I slept in the dark house; and, wouldn't you know it, that was the night Ben first climbed out of his crib and went wailing around the dark and messy basement trying to find us!

The house wasn't fully finished until November, but the pool and the backyard were done, so that's where we spent our days that summer while the various tradespeople worked their magic. Cindy and Rachel were a great help that summer, as they took the kids out on day trips and helped them get settled.

Life in Abbotsford was very full and mostly good. Pieter became busier with the business as he took leadership positions in national organizations such as CEMA (Canadian Egg Marketing Board) and CPEPC (Canadian Poultry and Egg Processors Council). This took him away to Ottawa a lot—sometimes, twice a month. They'd have meetings Monday and Tuesday. He'd have to fly out the day before, since we live in an earlier time zone. But that meant travelling on Sunday. This was not part of our church culture, since Sundays were to be set aside as days of worship, separate from the money-fuelled world of business. So, he would fly out Saturday afternoons, attend church services in Ottawa, and spend the rest of his Sunday sitting by himself in his hotel room, while I had to manage taking the kids to two services and all the rest of the busyness that Sundays brought. After a while, we admitted the ridiculousness, and he stayed home to go with us to our church Sunday mornings before he flew out. We were learning, bit by bit, to adapt our faith in an ever-changing world.

When he did come home Tuesday afternoons, he would often have to rush off to a consistory meeting where he was an elder, or a make a home visit to a church family to stay connected and supportive. Later in the week, the Men's Bible Study required his presence, too. At first, I tried to maintain some involvement in church life but soon found it next to impossible, so I was mostly keeping the home fires burning—or putting them out.

These were very busy years in every way. We had moved from the original, smaller business location, from the house Rika had built, and from the congregation that Pieter, Rika, his parents, and many of his siblings were members in. We had also moved from Surrey, a bedroom community that never felt like a neighbourhood. Now, we were still on the same property as the business, but it was a company that was in a big time of change, becoming more diverse in its products and its employee makeup. We were in a home I designed to fit a larger, more complex family, where the older children were reaching their adult years. We were actively part of setting up a new congregation in Aldergrove. And I loved Abbotsford. It had a community feel to it right from the beginning. People were friendly and relational. In many ways, it was a big step into our future.

# CHAPTER 26

## Schooling

In September, Phil and Mike divided their time between Trinity Western University and working at Vanderpol's. Cindy and Rachel were off to Credo Christian High, and Elsa and Margaret were enrolled in Credo Elementary (in second and first grade, respectively).

We had just moved into our home when our oldest son, Bill, called and said that he would like to move back home by Christmas and go to university. All the eight bedrooms were full, so we Velcroed a few walls into a corner of the recreation room, bought a wardrobe closet from IKEA, and made a personal space for him.

The days would begin with the chaos of getting them all fed and organized for school. I found a skit we'd done at Mike and Tina's wedding that may help paint the picture:

*Tonight, we are going to take you inside the walls of our home to share some of the day-to-day events that make up our family life. In recognition of your creative abilities, we have kept the props and costuming to a bare minimum, knowing that your imagination can complete the picture far more effectively than any attempts we could make to simulate reality.*

*Our scene takes place in the early morning hours in the Vanderpol kitchen. The sunlight is softly bathing a peaceful scene. The table has been set the night before in anticipation, waiting to be of service. The refrigerator is gently humming, but other than that there is nothing to disturb the cheerful early morning chorus of the finches and songbirds flitting about the windows. Then suddenly the hero appears. It is 6:52 a.m. The conscientious head of the household comes bounding into the kitchen, full of pep and energy after having completed his regimen of stretches and bends, raring to start the day right. He's tempted to pick up the phone to find out what's been happening in the business in Ontario—after all, they've been at it for three hours already—but, no… He must do what's important, not what is urgent. Keep your priorities straight! First, the family must be sent off with a nourishing breakfast. Bypassing the phone, he opens the fridge and pulls out two dozen eggs – packed full with all the essential nutrients, vitamins, and minerals every healthy body craves. Grasping three eggs in each hand, he efficiently cracks them, whips them, and, before you can mutter Canadian Inovatech, fluffy omelettes are simmering to perfection, the kettle is whistling merrily, and orange juice is glistening in the frosty jug. While he is busy with all of this, in bounces his faithful and exuberant assistant, Calvin.*

*"Can I help you make breakfast Dad?" he shouts in his booming voice. "I'm good at breaking eggs!" Oh, if only they were all so enthusiastic.*

*The clock says 6:59! Put out the alarm. "Breakfast time!" echoes and re-echoes throughout the house. One by one, in their own unique style, the family gathers around the table, mumbling their cheery good mornings. Elsa, dressed and reading a book. Margaret, sort of dressed and reading a book. Joni, not dressed but her hair is all fancy and she's reading a book. Then, up the stairs come two imposing figures wrapped in colourful robes—Bill and Phil. They are soon joined by more robed figures, as Cindy comes down the hall and then Rachel, head wrapped in a terrycloth turban and her nose in a book. Finally, Mom puts in her appearance after successfully emptying all the beds, carrying a still sleeping Benjamin, who gets propped up in his chair hoping he will wake up sometime before breakfast is over.*

*As the clock strikes seven, ten pairs of hands are folded, and ten heads bowed as the head of the household, after installing a fluffy omelette on each plate, takes his position at the head of the table. With one final look of inspection, he realizes that there should be eleven heads bowed. "Michael!" he shouts down the stairs. "Michael!" Shortly thereafter, sleepy steps are heard ascending the stairs, a grunt which we all accept as a warm greeting and the last chair is filled with yet another robed figure. Now, with twelve heads bowed, breakfast can begin.*

After breakfast, the mad competition for bathroom space, finding the right outfits for the day, and tossing all that was needed into backpacks, the doors would open. Six kids and Pieter scurried out, and I was left with the mess and the relative peace and quiet of three little ones.

Then, at around 4:00 p.m., the doors would open, and they would all reappear, hungry, tired, maybe frustrated or anxious, needing to do homework, run off to an after school job, or wanting to spend some time outdoors or with friends. In my spacious kitchen, I was busy cooking enough food for all of them and any friends that may have come along, while trying to hear about their days and deal with any issues that were going on. The toddlers entered piranha hour, as their hunger and tiredness became more and more evident. Juggling homework and story time after dinner, with a husband who also wanted to talk about his day before he had to head out to a meeting, made it very stressful. It looked and felt like chaos, yet somehow, it flowed, and things got done.

When summer came, the more relaxed pace felt so lovely. The children were so much happier and more relaxed, and, therefore, so was I. Little Marg, especially, had a very difficult time in grade one. She was in a very large class of thirty-eight students with a very soft-spoken teacher, and she had high anxiety. I couldn't face the thought of sending her off to school again.

That's why, one night, lying in bed, I shocked Pieter out of his drowsiness by saying, "Piet, I'm so busy and can't manage it all, so I'm thinking of homeschooling." He was totally mystified as to how this would in any way solve my problem until I explained my usual sound reasoning.

My daytime hours were relatively do-able. It was the before- and after-school ones that left me feeling like I wasn't meeting the needs of the family. If I could keep Elsa and Margaret home, I could spend time with them and not have to cater to Credo Elementary School's expectations. Our housekeeper could come in three days a week and do much of the laundry, cleaning, etc., so I could focus on the kids. Then, when the 4:00 p.m. rush came, I could, with a bit less guilt, send the little ones off to play and focus more on the older ones. He bought the story so, come September, I began my homeschool journey.

Back in the early nineties, homeschooling was a new, hippie-type thing. There were next to no resources or support, but I was reasonably confident that I could do it. I'd been there before in my teaching career. I ordered what resources were available, but for the most part, I was determined to be intentional about making every moment a learning opportunity. We read lots of books and listened to stories on tape when we were driving off to Science World or some other educational place. We learned to observe, imagine, and wonder. And we learned to read, write, work, and play with numbers. Besides, I kept assuring myself and others, it was only for a few years until our home life became a little less busy. Well, we homeschooled for ten years. As the others reached school age, they were added to the school routines until there were six around the kitchen table. They may have missed out on some finer points of curriculum and being part of school events. They also missed out on the peer pressures and classroom social structures. Instead, they built very close bonds with each other. To this day, these six children stay very connected and are each other's close friends.

Bill combined his studying at Trinity Western with his agriculture training and managed our dairy barn. We had built a barn on the property and dairy cows grazed in the fields to provide milk for the family and, more importantly, the business. The milk was used in our scrambled egg mixes. Bill had been the one back in Surrey to have the idea of starting a small dairy business with a few cows to supply the family's milk. Now, he was milking about a dozen cows. Morning and evening, he and some of his younger siblings would trudge off to the barn to do the chores. It was a great way for Bill to build bonds with them, and they loved the adventure. Little two-year-old Ben was a faithful companion in his little red rubber boots, waving a big stick to coax the cows into the barn while Cindy and Rachel helped with the real work.

The dairy barn eventually morphed into a horse barn so the girls could all, in their turn, get the fabulous experience of horse ownership. We started off with a smaller horse barn closer to the house so Cindy and Rachel could finally each buy their horse. Riding lessons and even a few horse shows were wonderful experiences before the increased social life of a sixteen-year-old with a licence and a part-time job made the horses less of a priority. The experience of owning a horse was very special and important during those years.

We had had a dairy barn in Surrey, with sheep, chickens, and even peacocks, rabbits and ducks. Well, we had the ducks for about a minute. When Pieter released them onto the pond that he had lovingly prepared for them, they promptly flew away, never to be seen again.

In Abbotsford, in addition to the cows and horses, we also had a donkey, miniature goats, chickens, rabbits, and, of course, always a faithful dog. There were also all manner of indoor pets, including cats, hamsters, gerbils, hedgehogs, hermit crabs, beta fish, and even a hairless rat that would crawl all over Joni's neck and arms.

*Can we be friends?*

*Joni and her bunny sharing love and carrots.*

Education has always been very important, including both the formal schooling and the rich experiences of living with people of all ages in an environment filled with animals and nature, business and community, books and resources. We had children from preschool to university all under one roof and gathered around one dinner table. It doesn't get richer than that!

# CHAPTER 27

## Becoming Grandparents

Norma had married Mike Kobald while we still lived in Surrey. They were living in Waterloo while Mike worked on his Engineering degree. Norma was expecting their first baby. Mike's Mom had said that she would fly out as soon as Norma was in labour so she could be there for them. *Great*, I thought. *I will let her share this special time with her first grandchild and then go out later.* But then baby Alex was born on the first Sunday in August, and Mike's Mom decided that she wasn't going to go right away. Piet looked at me and said, "Do you want to go?

"Do I?" I jumped out of my chair in excitement. Calvin was eleven months old, and then there was the rest of the family, but that didn't stop me. We made some quick arrangements, and early the next morning, I was on a flight to Ontario. I spent a lovely week bonding with our first precious grandchild, Alex, and built treasured memories with Norma and Mike.

Having a baby myself, the routines were all familiar. Actually, Norma was also very comfortable with babies, having helped welcome and care for so many siblings. She had been a great help and support to me when Elsa and the others were born, and now I got to return the favour. Having your own baby is a completely different experience than helping with someone else's, and I was so happy to help her through that first overwhelming week.

*Alexander Vincent Kobald - the first of the next generation.*

Norma's baby was the first of our many grandchildren. Our family was growing up. By the early nineties, we had four kids who had graduated from high school, pitching them headfirst into the new stage of adulthood, making career and life partner explorations and decisions. It required a whole new level of conversation, many held late at night, sitting on the kitchen counters. Five years after we had moved in, four more got married and moved out within a fourteen-month whirlwind.

Mike and Tina were the first to make that big step in June of 1994. This may have been a bit of a catalyst for Mark to propose to Cindy. Mike and Tina's wedding was where Phil first met Jenn, and they began dating not too much later. Mark and Cindy married in December, with a Christmas-themed wedding. Cindy was a very busy nursing student at the time, but they managed to pull it all together. Phil and Jenn married in March of 1995 and found a nice home nearby. Bill had met Amy singing in the choir at TWU, and since he was graduating that spring, they tied the marriage knot in August. Rachel graduated from high school in 1995 as well, so our life went through a lot of change.

A bit of the emptiness was filled when baby John, a late-life surprise pregnancy, enriched our family and moved into the nursery that September. The pregnancy had been challenging. I was forty-five years old, and I thought I was in menopause, yet here we were. My body was well aware of its age! Then, I also had to joyfully support and participate in Phil and Jenn's, and Bill and Amy's, weddings, on top of Bill's and Rachel's graduations, when I could hardly both stand up and sing at the same time in church. We cancelled a planned trip to Japan for that spring, and little Elsa went off to her big Pacific Mennonite Children's Choir concert tour to Germany without me that summer, but we made it.

John was born at 3:00 p.m. on Monday, September 18, 1995. We were home again by 6:30 p.m., surprising the rest of the kids during their dinner. Mike and Tina had stepped in to look after them all. Lying in bed that night with John securely tucked in between us, Piet and I felt so richly blessed and content.

Life carried on. Though the weekdays maybe had a slightly less chaotic routine, Sundays and special days now became times when the married ones would come visit, along with their babies and toddlers, and the house was once again full, noisy, and hectic. I loved it. It seems to be my happy state. It was an interesting mix of generations, since the older grandchildren and our youngest children were overlapping in ages. But, still having young children of my own made being a grandparent quite different than most people experience. I was still very busy managing a full household and immersed in babies and young children myself. The grandkids often were much more excited to come play with our younger children, who were their friends, than to visit us, their Opa and Oma.

*In front of our home in Abbotsford 1999*

# CHAPTER 28

## Leaving Our Church and Finding a New One

In January of 1999, we withdrew from our church. This was such a difficult and painful decision to make. We had both been born, baptized, and raised in this church community, and we had been very active participants. Though we had concerns and some different thoughts, we had never really considered leaving the church. There was room for different ways of thinking and living out the faith. Yet, now the circumstances locally convinced us that it was actually best for us and our younger children to find a new church home.

For Pieter and I, along with our pastor and a small group of other members, it was about remaining faithful to what the Bible teaches. To others, especially the leadership at the time, conforming to the traditions and expectations of the community seemed more important. Most members were uncomfortable with change and just wanted to live peacefully in the ways we had always done.

To be fair, Pieter and I had always been open and interested in reading, attending conferences, etc. that exposed us to other ways of understanding our faith, while many others preferred to stay within the traditions and authorities of the federation. Building upon our history of experiencing God working directly in our lives and actively exploring to know God better, we had probably changed considerably. But you don't so much see gradual change within yourself until you compare it with "the control group"—those who didn't have the same opportunities or desire to learn. We understood that it wasn't our business to make others change if they were happy where and as they were. We also saw that if we did decide to stay, we'd have to "keep our mouths shut" about a lot of things, so we wouldn't be able to fully participate the way we wanted to and had always done.

So, we withdrew. To complicate matters, Tim and Rachel had their wedding planned right around that time, so we had to do some quick adjustments. But we made it all work out. Those of our children who were adults were encouraged to stay and make their own decisions based on their own experiences. "This is our issue," we told them. "You should stay where you are and be active members. If and when you can no longer be that, you must make your own decisions." Bill and Amy had already left when they got married. Amy had been brought up in a Pentecostal Church, and they worked together to find a church that they would both be happy in. The others all remained where they were for various lengths of time, but gradually, one by one, they also left and found new church homes.

We were anticipating taking some time to explore the many churches in our city before settling somewhere. However, the second church we visited felt like home to us. Hillside Christian Reformed Church had the familiar doctrinal and traditional history of the Reformed faith but was breathing new life into it. Many of its members were educators in the Christian Schools, so we shared the same experience of reading the Bible and trying to apply its truth through the eyes of a child. Educators need to be visionary because they are laying the foundations that will influence how the next generation lives. You must always be questioning the reasons for, and foundations of, what you are doing and teaching. And educators actively search for creative and varied ways to teach, inspire, and live out those truths. The lesson isn't complete until the students are demonstrating that they understand it and are using it in further and wider ways.

This small group of believers firmly believed and lived out that every member matters and ministers. Every person present, male or female, child or adult, should feel like they matter, both to God and to the people in the room. Each person should carry what they need to help them in their day to day when they leave, whether it is comfort and peace, direction and inspiration, or community. And everyone could and should be an integral part of each worship service to their comfort level.

We all healed in this atmosphere of total acceptance and room to grow. Once healing began, we grew stronger in our faith and more daring in living it fully in ways that were not considered conventional in our former lives. I look back with amazement on how I grew to become more and more confident in exercising the leadership abilities I had. Pieter and I had always been readers and thinkers, willing to explore ideas, whether business, theology, or whatever else. But we always stayed fairly safe within the accepted culture we were in.

Now, we were exposed to an ever-wider circle of thinking, and we were challenged to apply our learning in very real ways. Lee and Ilean Hollaar, who were already becoming good friends, invited us to help them plan a service they were going to lead. This was a whole new experience for us, who had been used to a liturgy based style of service led exclusively by the officially designated and highly theologically educated pastor. It required a very careful examination of what we had always assumed to be correct. Pieter or I, or some of our children, would be asked to read a passage of scripture or a prayer. For me, a woman—one who had never been comfortable with, or needed to, get up in front of a group (other than my own classroom years ago)—it was a nerve-wracking but exciting opportunity.

Services did not need to follow a regular script, but they all declared the truth of the gospel in fresh new ways. Sometimes, it was a familiar liturgy with a three-point sermon; other times it could include dramas or activities designed to teach, inspire, or celebrate our joy.

Those opportunities gradually pushed me further out of my shell, forcing me to grow and learn. The church I grew up in had a closed Communion Table—only adults who had made Public Profession of their Faith in front of the Church Council and the entire congregation were invited and allowed to participate. Children watched and listened. In Hillside, Communion was open to all, and it was up to the parents how their children would participate. They also celebrated Communion often, not the formal four to six times per year that I was accustomed to. The first time we celebrated Communion with them, I told our kids that they couldn't participate. Nine-year-old Calvin wasn't happy, and the following week he presented his case. I mustered all my old arguments, and he knocked them down one by one. That's still his style. In the end, we both agreed that children could and should participate. So, they all did. When little four-year-old John celebrated his first communion with me, handing him a piece of the bread, explaining to him that Christ's body was for him, and he was part of it, I knew we had made a good decision.

Leaving the church community that we had grown up in was very painful. This was the community that had defined my life in so many ways; it had raised, supported, and sheltered me. I knew and loved its people and its truths. But we had grown beyond its walls and needed a new space to continue our growth. I will admit that initially, in my hurt, I was quite cynical and bitter, seeing all the glaring faults of my mother church. And, unfortunately, I did not hesitate enough to talk about it with family, friends, and even strangers. I think it was a necessary part of the change and healing process, but I'm sorry for the hurt and awkwardness it brought to family relationships and thankful that they tolerated it with love.

I did also recognize some of its strengths, including the Reformed doctrine and especially the strength of community. I also came to realize how our strengths can, at the same time, be our biggest threats when we do not continuously and honestly adapt and apply them to present realities. It's never enough to say that we have reformed. As my pastor used to say, we need to be continuously reforming. The structures, traditions, and practices that worked in a less educated, struggling immigrant society were not the most effective in a society of second- and third-generation Canadians living in a twenty-first-century, technological, and global society.

Thankfully, leaving the church did not break relationships with my family and Pieter's. It affected them, of course, but the love and belonging were still there. My Dad was still alive at the time. He never criticized me for leaving, though I'm sure it grieved him deeply. But, as he had always done, he respected and trusted me to make good decisions.

# CHAPTER 29

## Business: My Turn

Another leadership opportunity came a few years after we joined Hillside. In the 1990s, Pieter had joined with new partners, and they had grown and expanded the egg business to produce more complex innovative products. Canadian Inovatech, their partnership company, was all about innovative egg technology. We had begun with developing the process for extracting lysozyme back in the eighties, and that had opened our minds to so many other possibilities. We were now quite involved in international markets and complex technology. The huge dryers, no longer needed for egg powder, were now drying dairy products such as whey proteins. As so often happens when a small company becomes successful with an innovative product, there are opportunities to sell it off to a larger company. In 2002, we sold the international egg products division of the business and restructured the partnership.

Pieter's business life now looked quite different. He was left as the sole owner of the original flagship company, Vanderpol's Eggs Ltd, as well as the real estate and the dryers processing the whey protein powders. Phil was running the dairy business, and Rachel's husband, Tim, was managing the cold storage. Being in his sixties by then, Pieter didn't think it wise to take the helm of Vanderpol's Eggs again, so he planned to sell it to one of his employees. His succession plan originally had been to sell it to the employee share-owners, but that hadn't worked out as he had hoped. If you're interested to learn more about this, you can find the details in his book, *First with the Finest.*

Then, Piet's General Manager, Rick, wanted to buy the business. However, the plan was to buy fifty per cent now and the rest over the next few years. Pieter asked if I would be willing to take on the other fifty per cent and partner with him. He knew that it would be too difficult to change the boss/employee relationship he and Rick had had for twenty years. I had just enrolled the six younger kids in school and was looking forward to some actual free time during the day. I was also sure that I had zero business knowledge, so I said no. But he finally convinced me: "It'll just be a few hours once or twice a week to check in with Rick and hear how it's all going," he said. I supposed I could do that.

Pieter also saw that while Rick was very familiar with the business, especially from the finance and accounting perspective, he wasn't as great at building relationships and communications. He saw that strength in me and therefore wanted me to help the business succeed.

Well, I actually really enjoyed business and being out and working with people outside of my home and church. Soon, I was taking on projects and responsibilities and spending more and more time at the office during school hours. I learned that my fourteen years of teaching and many years of managing a family and household had equipped me with a lot of leadership skills. I took a few business leadership courses and found some good mentors to hone these skills and learn more business-specific knowledge.

Rick and I worked quite well together. During these years, Rick worked hard to set up a small operation in Airdrie Alberta to make use of Alberta eggs and serve their local markets. This smaller plant was also better suited to doing some innovative new projects. So, as Rick focused more on the Alberta projects, I became more and more involved in the BC production.

After a few years of this, it came to the point where, instead of Rick buying me out as planned, we separated the two operations, allowing each of us to focus on one. It was a bit messy and painful, I will admit, but we felt that it needed to be done. So here I was, in January 2005: a woman, homemaker, and owner and President of the flagship family business that had always been run by men. It was daunting. But I hung in there, taking more business management courses, joining business leader groups, and doing my best. Pieter fully supported me in this all. I also often felt Pieter's Dad beside me in my office, encouraging me and reminding me of the values he had instilled in the business.

Pieter was trying very hard to help me succeed, and he had his ideas on how to do that. His ways were not my ways, and as much as I tried, I couldn't understand his ways well enough to even attempt them. This led to a lot of stress, anxiety, and conflict. For the first twenty years of our marriage, we never fought. We had such a similar value system and faith life that we generally agreed on most things or could talk them out. Moreover, we had a fairly clear division of labour, where we knew who played the lead and who was the support in different areas and times. Now, it seemed to me that we were disagreeing a lot. It was such a stressful and difficult time for us and our children. The stress of learning to run a business on top of not seeing eye-to-eye with the one who had been a founder was huge.

I got through this, one day at a time, by reading and rereading my Mom's favourite Psalm: "Whoever dwells in the shelter of the Most High will rest in the shadow of the Almighty." I needed to stay in God's shelter to be able to rest in His shadow. This constant reminder that it was not about me helped me keep sanity and perspective. I was there as a very real participant. Yet, the bigger picture was that it was God doing His work. The same God who had brought Pieter and I together twenty-five years before was also, and equally, present in this. It was very difficult and very messy, but renovations, whether of buildings, businesses, or souls, require a messy deconstruction before you can begin to build something better. Sleepless nights would find me reading this Psalm over and over until I felt calm enough to sleep.

One day, we were standing in the kitchen yelling at each other. He was standing in front of the fridge making dinner when he shouted, "Are you going to leave me?"

And I shouted back, "No! I promised till death do us part, and I'm sticking to that!"

And he shouted back, "Me too!"

That voice inside my head said with a sly smirk, "You just renewed your marriage vows."

It took a while, but one day, Pieter came home and said, "You have no one to talk to, do you?" And it was too true. I didn't want to talk to the kids, our friends, or our church, because they're *his* kids, *his* friends, and *his* church. I did have a group of fellow entrepreneurs, the CENTS group (Christian Entrepreneurs), from whom I did receive some valuable support, but for the rest, I tried to struggle it out inwardly. That day, he suggested I call in someone to help us.

I called David Bentall. The Bentall Group in Vancouver was also a family business that had gone through much pain, and David wanted to be able to use the lessons they had learned to help others. David came out within a week, gave me a big hug, and got us to look at each other and begin to talk. Of course, it wasn't just between Pieter and me. The sons in the business also had their ideas and ambitions and me owning and running Vanderpol's was not part of it. This wasn't helping the situation, and Pieter was caught in the middle. So, we began to talk. We invited all of the children to help shape a plan for the future that would be transparent, fair and supportive of the various dreams and ambitions.

There was already a group of companies that included two operating companies and a holding company. The holding company, Vanderpol Enterprises Inc., owned all the land and buildings and some of the equipment of our previous three locations in Abbotsford (BC), St. Marys (ON), and Winnipeg (MB). Vanderpol's Eggs, which I now fully owned, was the egg processing operation. Then, Pieter owned Brookside Cold and Dry, which dried whey and milk proteins and provided cooler and freezer space for the egg and dairy operations, as well as some external customers.

Phil was running the drying or dairy business, and Tim the cold storage. Mike, at the time, was working for Michael Foods, who had bought our international egg division. Phil, Mike, and Tim were all bright and energetic young men, with their own young and growing families. They had learned the business from many years of working in it, and they were ready—chafing at the bit you could say—to have something of their own.

I'm so proud of our family. Pieter and I proposed that over the next few years, all of the children would collectively take over Vanderpol Enterprises and its assets. We decided that this was one of the ways we could leave a legacy rather than just a financial inheritance. We could work together as parents and children for a while, with the second generation taking over more of the responsibility and decision-making as they, and we, felt comfortable. At the time, the children ranged in age from forty-five to twelve, so it was a huge spread.

Those discussions were full of visionary thinking and love for one another and beyond. Together, we explored the benefits and responsibilities of ownership and wealth. "We're all capable of looking after ourselves and our families," they said. "But it would be nice to be able to use some of our wealth to help others and build family relationships."

They were well aware of the potential for challenges and strife in working together. They also understood the extra work and commitment that would be required. Many of them were busy enough with their own young families, as well as building their own careers. Yet, they agreed to go forward together.

Phil, Mike, and Tim then asked to buy the operating businesses. They had a vision of potentially running all the operations together in some form of partnership. This was discussed among the whole group, and we all agreed that we would be very happy to see each of them succeed. We gave them our full support for their success.

Pieter didn't want to sell the dairy business at the time because it needed a lot of work in a changing marketplace to reach its potential, but he would hand over management to Phil, Mike, and Tim. So, they bought Vanderpol's Eggs from me, and Brookside Cold Storage from Pieter, at a fair market value and began their new adventure.

It was a huge learning and growing curve for each of them, including all of the stresses and pains that are a necessary part of growth. We had created a Board of Directors consisting of qualified professionals outside of the family to provide help and support and keep Pieter and I, and the rest of the family, from interfering in the business. This would, hopefully, allow us to keep family relationships separate from business. However, it's very difficult to do that. Emotions seep through cracks. So, unfortunately, some relationships became strained and distant.

Vanderpol Enterprises (VEI) became the family-owned and managed company. It owns the land and buildings on which our companies operated in Abbotsford, St. Marys, Winnipeg and Chilliwack. It is a corporation run by a Board of Directors consisting of family members and outside directors with particular expertise. Its first years have been devoted to paying down debt, so we didn't feel any tension over how to "spend" the profits. However, from its beginning, funds flowed into the Oikodome Foundation, which Pieter and I had set up in 1992. This Foundation deserves its own chapter, so for now, I will only say that it has been a passion of ours for most of our married life, and we also are happy to share it with our children.

VEI has been a blessing in many ways. It provides a great hands-on business and leadership learning opportunity for everyone. It also provides a common purpose and shared experiences that help keep the family together. There are two committees that family members can sit on. The Business Committee oversees the business, providing training and hands-on experience. The Family Committee plans regular family retreats, as well as supporting any family needs. They connect with grandchildren as they leave high school to offer support, mentorship, and post-secondary tuition assistance.

Some of the profits are used for family retreats. Many good memories were built in our extended weekends at Middle Beach Lodge in Tofino, on Vancouver Island's far west coast, to celebrate Pieter's milestone birthdays. We have great memories of surfing the waves, trekking into town for a brewery and distillery tour, having family photos taken on the beach, and enjoying delicious meals together in the cozy lounge and dining areas.

*Family photo shoot at Middle Beach Tofino.*

*Pieter launched his book "First With The Finest" on his 80th birthday. A great opportunity to pass on family history and the values that shaped it.*

*Cal, Pieter J, and Colin immersed in their copies.*

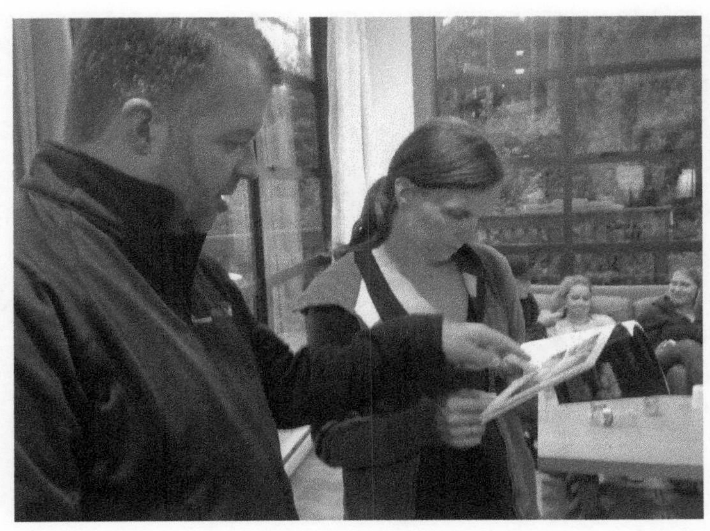

*Phil explaining some details to Marg.*

TOFINO
BREWING

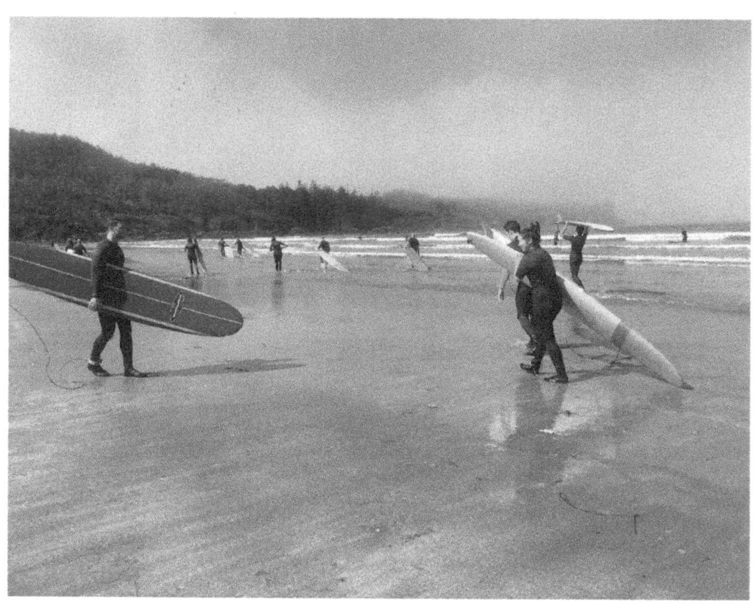

We also spent a Christmas in California! We had lots of fun squeezing freshly picked oranges from the trees outside the door for breakfast and languishing in the pool as the kids splashed cool but sunny afternoons away. These retreats are great fun, and they are very important ways to bond and have fun as a group and as individuals. Hopefully, these will continue after Pieter and I are gone.

*Many hands make light work and lots of fun. Tina (on the right) gets the credit for organizing this wonderful Christmas adventure.*

*The whole crew in front of our California 'home for the holidays'*

Mixing family relationships and business is hard. So many of the tensions are caused by past hurts and unexplored and unexamined assumptions that may or may not be related to the actual business itself. I'm confident that each family member shares many important values and similar vision, and I know they're all great people. I try to keep my focus on how working together creates opportunities and is a learning and growing experience for us all. Hopefully, we build enough good memories and create enough advantages to counterbalance the more difficult aspects. It's messy and scary, and it's not for the faint of heart. But we're a determined bunch who have the potential to create something good.

My eyes are also on the third generation, our precious grandchildren. They are such a gifted and diverse group. If we can help shape their identity as being part of a family that can work together, support one another, and intentionally work at making our world a better place, I will be content. I will know that it has all been worth all the effort.

# CHAPTER 30

## Abbotsford: My City

Pieter and I now entered another stage of life. I was retired from business, and most of the kids were adults and quite independent. For some years, we had only John at home. So, I had some free time again.

That's when the "books of judgment" that I talked about earlier opened. Now, for probably the first time since I'd married Pieter, I had lots of time to think and process what had happened over the years. It was not easy. Our children were now parenting their own and doing a pretty good job of it—much better than I remember doing. As I witnessed their patience and their ability to focus on each child's uniqueness and needs, I wondered if we had made a huge mistake in having such a large family. Did I do great harm because I was not able to provide enough one-on-one, focused attention? Did my busyness and stresses have negative impacts on their development? Did I really understand any one of them well enough? Hurtful words I had spoken in anger or ignorance were echoing in my ears. Missed opportunities to better understand and support them could not be retrieved. I was painfully aware of my ignorance, naiveté, and shortcomings. We tend to dwell on our imperfections. I needed a Brené Brown back then, but I didn't find her TED talks and books until later.

There were also many good things that I was extremely thankful for. Pieter and I sometimes say, "What would our family and our life be like if we, both Pieter and Rika and Pieter and I, had only had two children? Imagine a family with Norma, Bill, and, much later, Elsa and Margaret. How would our family and our community be if there were no Phil, Mike, Cindy, and Rachel? No Joni, Ben, Cal, and John? It would be vastly different. Each one of us, our characters and lives, have been shaped by being a part of the whole. Like pebbles on a beach, our rough edges have been worn smoother. Each one is now grown, and our family has been enriched by many sons and-daughters-in-law, as well as grandsons and granddaughters. They are all making important contributions in so many and varied ways, adding another dimension of richness.

Of course, I also doubted my business involvement. Had I just made a huge fool of myself in trying to do something that I was not really capable of doing? I felt like a fool that had rushed in where angels know better than to tread—trying to provide leadership in a man's world. My leadership intuitions were forged in a classroom of children and in trying to meet the needs of my family. Had I hurt family relationships by entering the men's sphere of business? By neglecting a mother's responsibility of devoting all her energies to her husband and children? Instinctively, I knew that this was not only untrue, but that the business had been more successful than I, or anyone else, seemed to want to give me credit for. I had successfully run the business and made it profitable. I had nurtured a community, encouraged teamwork and cooperation, and worked hard to develop a strong vision and identity for the company.

I recall that one day when I was running the business, I was rushing out the door and one of the kids said, "Bye Mom, thanks for visiting. Come again soon." I stopped in my tracks. Later, I asked my children if I should just quit and come back home. My daughters said, "No, Mom. You are teaching us that women and girls can do these things. You are showing us that nothing is impossible and to not be afraid to try!" I was so grateful for their wisdom.

An interesting development that came out of my business ownership experience was a greater involvement in our local community. With my business experience and connections, I had enough confidence and credibility to step out of the walls of my house again. With a group of local Christian business leaders, we started a group called Fusion. We planned a number of events, inviting local leaders in all areas to speak to us or join a panel on how we, as Christians, could use our skills and opportunities to get outside of the walls of our churches and build a stronger local community. I was surprised at the amount and quality of support and interest we got, proving that there are a lot of Christians with a passion and mission to do good within and for their city. We did this for a year or so, and then Fusion got incorporated into Power2change. This was a much larger international organization, and I stepped back.

Abbotsford is a great community, often referred to as the buckle of the Fraser Valley Bible Belt. It has over one hundred churches of many denominations with an especially large Mennonite and Reformed influence. There is also a large Sikh community with its temples and school. But the sadness of it is that faith communities tend to stay within their own walls and silos. Abbotsford continually tops the list of charitable giving by far, yet most of the money stays within the faith communities or is sent overseas. We have programs and projects that involve and support our own yet, in so many ways we are naïve to the many real and hurtful struggles both within and outside of our walls. Our faith teachings and traditions teach us to love our neighbours and welcome the strangers but, when we get right down to it, that is very hard work, messy and costly. So, we do the parts that we can more easily manage and support the few that are willing to get their hands dirty and their hearts broken. This way we remain neat and clean, at arms length from the real pain, while reassuring ourselves that we are doing what we can.

We suffer the consequences of broken and hurtful relationships, seeing their effects in such things as addictions, homelessness, suicide, violence, gangs and crime. Tragically, we had a gang and drug problem that was ruining or taking the lives of many of our young people. In 2007 and 2008, we had the distressing title of being the murder capital of Canada. The Abbotsford School District agonized over this. These were our students—otherwise good kids getting, often naively, sucked into the drug and gang world. Why didn't these kids see the threats? Why couldn't they say no? The schools started being very intentional about teaching values and virtues, beginning in preschool.

However, they also believed that it was important that the whole community become involved, providing a consistent message, standards, and support to our children. They invited a small group of community leaders to discuss this, and Pieter and I, alongside some others, volunteered to help out.

Since I had the most free time, I took it upon myself to promote this concept to key community leaders. In April

2011, we held a forum of about seventy community leaders, including the Mayor and City Councillors, the Police Chief and officers, business leaders, faith leaders, and community organizations. Together, we came up with a list of six character values we all agreed were important, and we agreed to integrate and promote them within our organizations and spheres of influence. These values are respect, responsibility, integrity, empathy, courage, and service. Character Abbotsford was born.

For the first few years, it was called Abbotsford City of Character, but then we did a branding exercise and changed the name. This table of leaders still meets regularly to support and encourage one another and organize public events, such as a large, well-attended annual conference and a Youth Forum for middle and secondary students. I remained involved with them until 2017, when I felt I had contributed what I could and it was time to make room for others around the table.

I had learned to stretch myself again, way beyond my comfort zone, and I met so many wonderful, visionary people of all ethnicities, faiths, and professional spheres. It was such an enriching and encouraging experience seeing how much goodness there is in so many people and how their leadership and influence shapes our community.

Early on, when I was trying to get the character movement going, Pieter and I had attended the Mayor's Breakfast, where Mayor George Peary had done an excellent job highlighting what was happening in the city. A few days later, we ran into him at another public event. Piet knew him through business, so they stopped to chat. Suddenly, I awkwardly blurted out, " I really enjoyed your presentation at the breakfast. But next year, you need to talk about the importance of character!" Both the Mayor and I were very surprised at my uncharacteristic outburst, but he took it graciously. The following year, Mayor

Peary's address to the city was filled with stories of how people showed their good character and were enriching and influencing our city.

Character Abbotsford was a very challenging project, especially because character is such a broad, undefined concept. Yes, you can come up with a list of shared character attributes. Yes, you can organize a few events or set up some programs. But how does a city become a city of character? I had no simple or concrete answers. Many times, I thought to myself, "Just drop this 'baby' in a corner and walk away." Every time I would try to do that, within a day or two, someone, even people I only vaguely knew, would come up to me and say, "You know that character work you're doing? Don't give up on it! We need it." What could I do but go back to that corner and pick the baby up again?

One important benefit and struggle, from this experience was that I had to learn to speak another language. For most of my adult life, I had lived in the Reformed Christian bubble, and I spoke that Christianeze with a Reformed accent quite well. Expressions like, "Let's pray about it," or "The Bible says," would not be very effective when speaking to people of other, or no faith. So, I had to learn to speak my truths in a language they would understand and accept. At first, I wondered if I was maybe betraying God by not openly using His name or quoting Scripture verses; I worried that I was 'watering down' my beliefs.

But when I began to translate my Christianeze, I also had to do some much deeper thinking. The platitudes and shortcuts that I was familiar with wouldn't work, and quoting a Scripture passage didn't have the authority it does within the church community. I realized that these were often shortcuts that did not require us to fully understand the concepts. Suddenly, I needed a deeper understanding and a different language to convey what truth and ultimate authority are. Instead of making me doubt my faith, it actually made it all so much more amazing. I developed a much deeper understanding of some of the truths I had been taught, and I had a better grasp of some of what had previously been talked about only as mysteries beyond our understanding. This made it easier to apply Jesus' teachings to my everyday life and see how it is all unfolding in the world around us.

Another benefit of my Character Abbotsford experience was that I paid a lot more attention to my own character. How did each of these character traits—which we were asking people to think about and promote in their own organizations—really play out in the details of my own life? Respect. Responsibility, Integrity, Empathy. Courage. Service. Often, I would be merrily going along when I would pull myself up short and ask whether my action was indeed respectful of all people around me. Truth be told, I first needed to actually see them, to try to understand how they would perceive my actions and me. This meant greater empathy. Was I willing to take responsibility for my neighbours? What could that look like for me? Did I live as though all of life was truly integrated, or did I have my silos of family, church, work, and city? Was I stuck in silos of theory and theology, and practice and habits? Do I have the courage to speak up and speak out, to try things and be awkward? Of course, this all also extends to our physical environment—animals, trees, air and water.

These years and experiences were life changers for me. I now deeply know that I am not just Fran—female, Dutch immigrant, Christian, wife, mother, and grandmother. I am still Fran, but now I see myself as a person, a global citizen whose everyday life has opportunities to be a part of making this world a place of flourishing. I am still even Fenny, connected to my Opoe and my ancestral roots and extended family on both sides of the ocean. I am still female, raised in a patriarchal culture, trying to live more fully as an egalitarian while holding my complementarian residue with understanding, respect, and a recognition that while you can learn and embrace new ideas, it takes a while for the body, habits, and emotions to adapt. I am fully Canadian, and I am actively participating in a diverse, multicultural, multi-ethnic, democratic nation that is, hopefully, beginning to deal with its settler colonial history. I am still Christian, though my understanding of what that looks like has, as it should, matured considerably. And I'm still a wife, mother, and grandmother. These labels help define me and give me place and context. Mostly, I'm an image bearer of God, a vessel through which the love and truth of Jesus can flow freely.

# CHAPTER 31

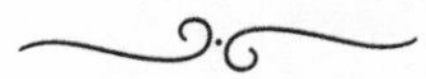

## Exploring Our Globe

As a young single person, I had travelled to learn more about Holland, the country of my birth and Canada, my home country. I had also travelled throughout Europe. These were fun adventures with adult friends..

After we married it became all about the family – what would the kids enjoy? How can we build family memories and relationships and have fun together. Pieter and I continued the summer camping trips with the family, usually ending up in Smithers to enjoy time with the VanDyk aunts, uncles, and cousins there. We'd hook up the trailer, load it full, and be off to enjoy exploring forests, cold lake swims, and roasting marshmallows over the campfire. These are precious memories! Sometimes, we'd end up in Alberta to visit relatives in the Coaldale area. We had a number of VanDyk reunions, in Smithers and Taber and the Fraser Valley. These were always very special times to renew family ties. Once we even made it all the way across to Ontario to be part of a Harsevoort family reunion.

Pieter and I also did some business travels together. We travelled across Canada to attend business conferences that were hosted in a different province each year. Later, we began attending international conferences that took us to such exotic places as Capetown, South Africa; Vienna, Austria; Santiago, Chile; Cyprus; and Bergen, Norway. These national and international conferences exposed us to these places from a bit of a different perspective than a cost-conscious young person would see. Four- or five-star hotels, guided excursions, and local entertainment allowed for some memorable experiences. I enjoyed the travel but found it so difficult to leave the family behind. Thankfully, we were always able to find someone to care well for them, but I could never get back home quickly enough. Sometimes, we took some of the kids along with us. The girls came along to Holland, and the boys to Chile.

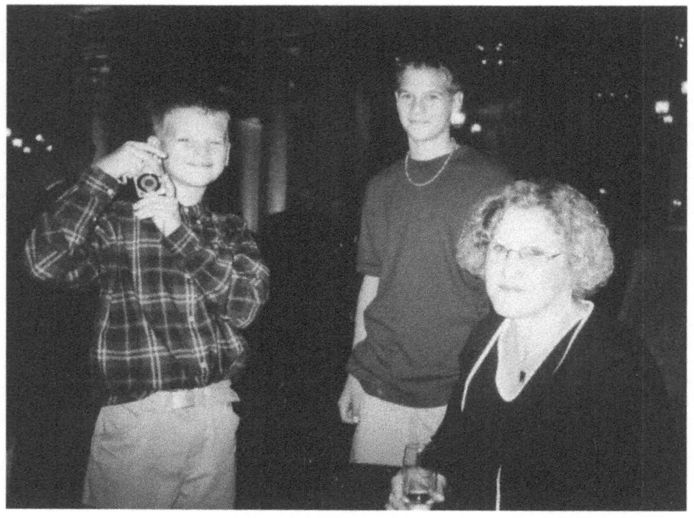

*Photographer Cal and Ben and I enjoying the special events in Chile.*

Apart from business and local travels, we also enjoyed some other adventures. One December, we sailed the waters around the British Virgin Islands with the married couples. Another summer, we did a Boat and Bike tour through western Holland with most of the kids, visiting the major cities. Delft, the place Pieter was born, and a side trip to Goeree Overflakee, where Rika came from, were highlights. A celebrated memory was when Jake took Marg up to the top of the tower of the church in Delft to propose to her. That evening, the dinner conversation consisted of older siblings conferring their blessing along with words of wisdom from their own experiences.

*Group photo in front of the Sarah that took us around the western part of Holland on our Boat and Bike Tour.*

*Piet was proud to show his children the place where he lived as a child. The original housing block had been replaced by this time.*

*Marg and Jake celebrating their engagement in Delft.*

We all went on a cruise to Alaska for our twenty-fifth anniversary, an exciting and memorable trip. The glamour and endless food and entertainment were so exciting, especially for the younger children and grandchildren.

When John was quite young, he expressed a strong wish to go to Israel to see the places where the Bible stories he loved had taken place. I promised him that I would take him when he was older, maybe twelve or thirteen, and then I filed that promise in the back of my head somewhere. On his twelfth birthday, as I wished him a happy birthday, he remembered the promise I had made years before and responded with, "When are we going to Israel?" The next morning, when I got up, he was studying Jerusalem on Google Maps. When he was thirteen, we finally made it there, with my youngest sister, Margaret, joining us. We stayed with our son-in-law, Mike's brother. Peter Kobald and his wife Chaya were living in Beersheba and were wonderful hosts. We spent the first week exploring the Negev Desert in Israel and the Wadi Rum in Jordan. Then we toured the north, Galilee, and finally Jerusalem. The highlight was watching John enjoy and explore to his heart's content.

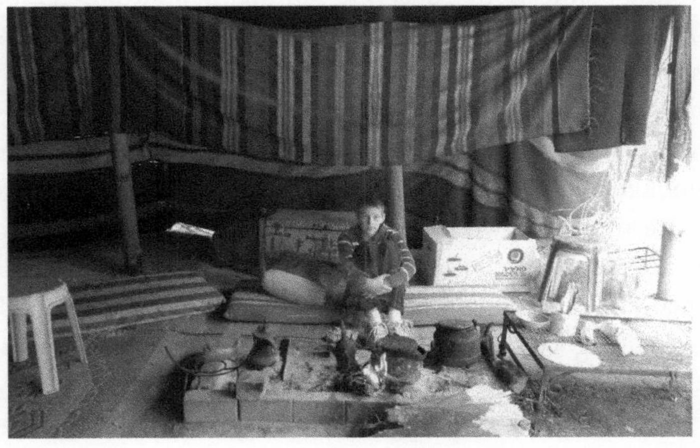

*John enjoying a tea ceremony in a Bedouin tent.*

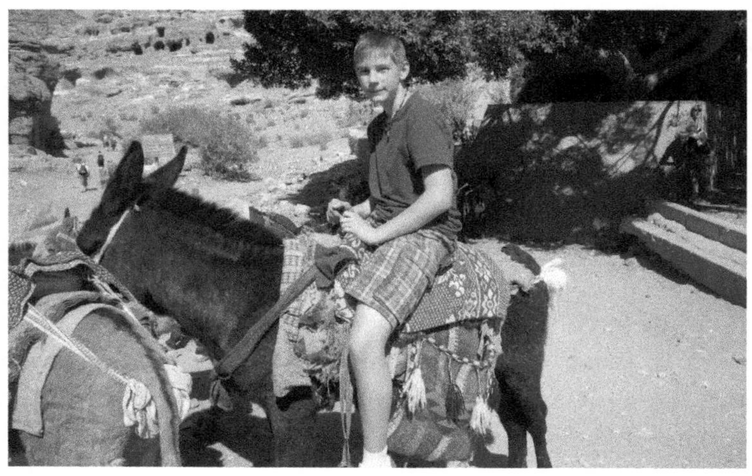

*John on a mule ride through Petra, Jordan.*

I also did other travel. Neither of us are the cruise or resort king of tourists, but we did dabble in these experiences. We prefer going somewhere with a purpose, usually including a personal connection. Thus, one summer, I went off to Liberia in Africa. We stayed with friends, James and Kathleen Ngenda, who were missionary community developers in Monrovia. James and Kathleen's son, Joshua, was a part of our family for a number of years when he came to Canada to further his high school education, so I accompanied him when he went home for the summer. Two professional educators who had a vision for helping less developed nations access better education joined us. Our Oikodome Foundation funded their trip. This was such a good trip for many reasons, and it certainly was an eye-opener for me on our privilege.

We made valuable connections with educators and top government officials to explore their needs and see if we could support them in any way. During the last days, we had a trip planned to go up-country. One of my co-travellers expressed disappointment that we had not had the opportunity to meet the President, Ellen Johnson Sirleaf. I said that our presence and purpose were well enough known around the capital city, so if she wanted to meet with us, we would hear. So, we went on our way. That night, after we had all retired to our hotel rooms, James got us all out in the hallway because someone was asking if we could meet with President Johnson Sirleaf the next afternoon. We revised our plans and were on our way back to Monrovia the next morning. We met with her in the afternoon. Unfortunately, it was a meeting that included a number of other foreign delegations, so we didn't get a lot of time to make our presentation. But we did get to see her and offer our assistance. And I received a signed copy of her memoir. Unfortunately, not too long after we were there, many of the connections we had made (e.g., with the Minister of Education) were reassigned to other positions, so nothing tangible came from the trip.

Another time, Pieter and I went to Panajachel, Guatemala, where friends through church were doing a very interesting program with Mayan youth from the outlying villages. Mayan children suffer a lot of discrimination and are discouraged from getting much education. They are lucky if their parents allow them to finish the required six years of schooling. Many must put up quite a "fight" to be allowed to go on, especially the girls. They live in poverty and ignorance, with much abuse and despair. Dave and Danaya MacDonald take their young family there year after year to mentor and teach some of these young people during their two-month school break in November-December. They tutor them in Spanish and English, but the most amazing change they bring about is in instilling self-worth and hope. They build a strong community, by intention and example, where every person matters and no one is left behind. These kids have grown from shoeshine boys and tortilla makers to winning scholarships to American Universities and finding jobs in technology, etc. I've built relationships with a number of them, following them through their growth from shy, oppressed, often abused children into confident, skilled adults who are the new leaders and role models in their communities.

*Evelyn took us to her home to experience the day to day life of Mayans in Guatemala. Her mother is a gifted weaver (as is Evelyn) who weaves the cloth that makes up the traditional dress using patterns typical to this village. I got to enjoy the full experience here.*

A few years ago, I had the privilege of visiting Vietnam. Two of our beautiful grandchildren were born there. They were both handed over at birth to a local orphanage by parents who, for some reason or another, couldn't care for them and were hoping that someone else could provide a better life. I can't imagine the heartache, for both the mother and the child. Marg and Jake were painfully aware of the needs of these orphans, so they went through the lengthy, painful, and expensive process of adopting first one child, Grace, and then another child from the same orphanage, Mae. When they finally got to go pick up Mae, they couldn't bear to have their family separated for the three weeks it takes, so Joni and I offered to accompany them and help with taking care of the now five children. We didn't do a lot of the tourist activities, but we sure got an appreciation for a gentle and kind nation of people. Their family and ours are so much richer with these two beautiful souls.

*Hanging out with the grandkids in VietNam*

*An outing to a farm in VietNam. It included cooking lessons and the delight of sampling these healthy all natural dishes. We also got water buffalo rides.*

We've done a few more touristy trips as well. Benji was living in Australia, making lots of new friends and adventures, so we decided to see what he was up to. We rented a two-bedroom apartment by Coogee Beach. It was big enough to host him and his friends, and we had a wonderful time.

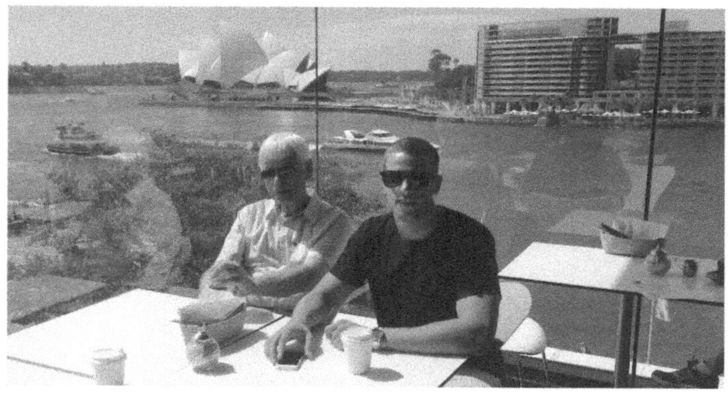

*Pieter and Ben enjoying coffees in Sydney.*

*Our apartment in Sydney overlooked Coogee Beach. A gorgeous and very convenient location.*

*Such a magnificent city to explore.*

Phil and Jenn went with us to Japan for a memorable adventure. We explored Tokyo, Kyoto and Hiroshima. It was such an interesting experience, from the unique, delicious and healthy cuisine to a culture quite different from ours. Touring Hiroshima was a very painful but eye-opening experience. We saw the horrors, but also the transforming effect it has had on Japanese and global politics.

*Getting the full treatment in Japan with Phil and Jenn. So many good memories.*

*This helicopter took Norma and Mike and Pieter and me across the mountains to the rainforest side of Costa Rica.*

We enjoyed Costa Rica along with Norma and Mike, amazed at the variety of landscape and vegetation. It was a fun trip that included a helicopter tour across a volcano to visit the rainforest part of Costa Rica. Unfortunately we didn't get to go too close to the volcano since it wasn't deemed safe.

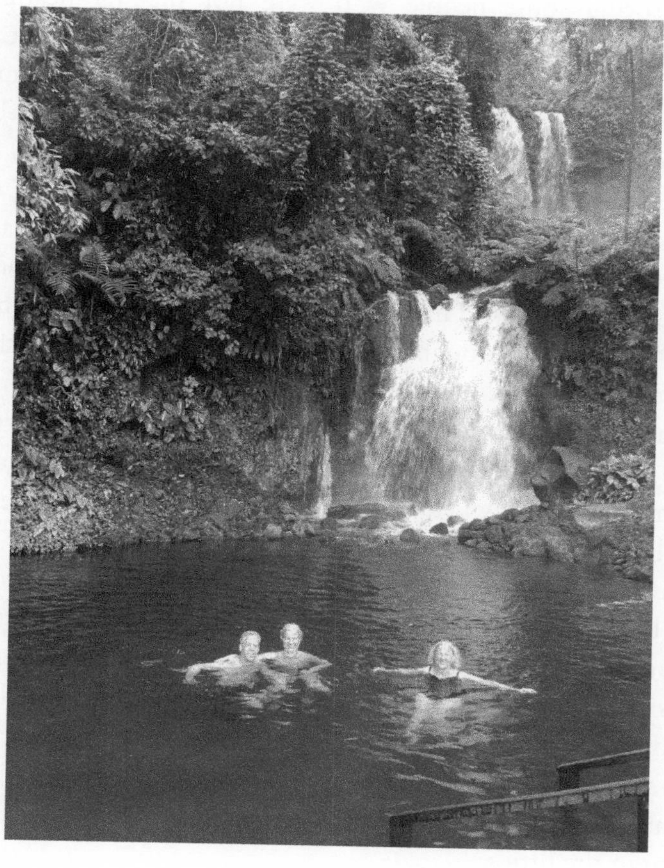

*Enjoying a refreshing dip during our rainforest hike.*

We didn't have to leave home to get a window into the effects of totalitarian regimes and persecution. When the Syrian tragedy was front-page news, a group from our church decided we wanted to offer help in sponsoring refugees. Our local MCC (Mennonite Central Committee) was able to provide the help and support we needed. However, they urged us to consider sponsoring some people who were not making headlines. Many people were ready to sponsor families, especially Syrians, as their tragic circumstances made news headlines for many months. Meanwhile, there were many single men languishing in camps in Africa that no one was paying attention to, so they were becoming hopeless. I had seen many healthy young men wandering the streets of Monrovia, Liberia, years before, and I had feared what could happen if the wrong powers got control of this frustrated and hurting group. Would we consider them?

We did and brought over our first group of five single Eritrean men. Suddenly, we had to become somewhat familiar with the geography, history, and culture of this country we had never really heard of before. It was an adventure! Each of them had their own stories and hopes, and we all did the best we knew how. A year later, they were all 'settled' with jobs, housing, and the beginnings of English. MCC came back to us, begging us to sponsor more, since the need was still so great, so we brought over another group of four single men. It is satisfying to see these men build new lives here. It is the land of opportunity, but it still takes time and a lot of effort, the same way we had to adapt as new immigrants. It's nice to be able to pay forward the help and support that we benefited from in the fifties.

People seek out people of their familiar culture, so, through our direct sponsors, we became connected with others from Eritrea. Now, we enjoy many friends and adopted children and grandchildren, and we get to enjoy their food and celebrations. For us, Canada Day now means an Eritrean Canadian barbecue with lots of fellowship, fun, and, of course, a banquet of food.

*No celebration is complete without a coffee ceremony.*

*Celebrating Canada day with our new Canadian friends and family.*

*Christmas celebrations*

The privilege of being able to travel and have first-hand experience of many cultures, climates, and landscapes has enriched me so much. Each place has its own beauty. Yet, as the airplane approaches Vancouver International, I still say to myself that home is the most beautiful of them all.

People are people. We are beautiful, friendly, and good. We all generally want the same basic things—to live peacefully in a healthy community. We want to see our children and our elderly healthy and cared for, with satisfied stomachs and peaceful minds.

This can only happen when we, as one global community, address the issues that stand in the way of flourishing. The diversity of cultures and faiths all have some wisdom and perspective to add to the conversation. We need to respect and care for our earth, learning from it, and living in harmony rather than exploitation. We truly need to love our neighbour—each and every one. When we have the courage to examine our assumptions, systems, cultural beliefs, and securities, and we are willing to pay the costs, in time and money, to pivot them away from self-service and protection toward caring about the big *us*, we can do so much better. For me, as a Christian, these are very Biblical truths—the heart of the message of Jesus. You can also say this in the language of other faiths, or in the language of humanity. Let's become multilingual and just do it!

# CHAPTER 32

## Theology and Arts

Regent College in Vancouver has been a gift to both Pieter and me. We began attending summer public lectures back in the eighties, where we were exposed to theologians and thinkers from various denominational backgrounds. We have taken courses that certainly stretched and deepened our knowledge and thinking. Some were focused on Bible study, while many more were about applying Biblical thinking to life's practices, especially the marketplace and the community.

Joni went on to get her Masters at Regent, a step on her journey that prepared her for her chosen vocation of being a Spiritual Care Practitioner.

In 2010, Regent offered a ten-session course called ReFrame. The premise is that we need to go back over the familiar stories our lives are built on to make sure that we truly understand them properly. Each session had a lesson delivered by a theologian providing a big-picture scope of a section of the Bible or

Church History. They were accompanied by presentations by other people who were practising their faith and understanding in creative and practical ways. Then, we were challenged to discuss some very thoughtfully prepared questions with a small group around a table. Later, these sessions were fine-tuned and filmed for a broader distribution.

I had the opportunity to be a part of the filming of the eighth episode that focused on how we impact our communities. I was already heavily involved in Character Abbotsford, so it was great fun to spend a few days filming in our home and around the city. I had the opportunity to talk about Pieter and my passion to live out our faith in every part of our lives, including our business and city. The film crew followed me around as I toured them around the city and participated in meetings. ReFrame has been shown in many groups locally and worldwide, and it has been translated into various languages.

Another organization that has had a lot of influence, challenging my stereotypes and encouraging much deeper thinking, is Pacific Theatre. Pacific Theatre is a Vancouver Live Theatre company, founded and run by a Christian and Regent College grad. It continues to challenge, stretch, inform, and afflict the comfortableness in me, even after many years of attending almost all of their live dramas. It has shown me time and time again the power of the arts to reflect our culture back to us. Theatre confronts us with the important questions and issues; in their complexity, they challenge us to deal with them in new and fresh ways.

These are the two that stand out for me. However, there were so many ways that I have grown and developed. Books have particularly helped me in this respect. We have had to pare down our library a number of times, but it keeps creeping back up. I find it difficult to resist bookstores or the convenience and availability of online ordering. In our technological world, there are also many blogs, podcasts, websites, etc. that keep me up to date by delivering regular contributions to my embarrassingly overflowing inbox. Our world is changing so rapidly, and it is exciting to watch, learn, and be a part of it.

# CHAPTER 33

## Oikodome

I briefly introduced our family Foundation but now I'll go into a bit more of the story. Somewhere in the mid-eighties, Pieter said that the business was doing comfortably well and no longer needed all the profits to be reinvested to build it up. "So, where do you think we should invest some money?" he asked.

I said, "Let's invest it in people." He quickly agreed, and that became our guiding principle. Very quickly, we became aware of opportunities to do just that.

When our children were graduating from high school, we needed to become more familiar with the opportunities and needs of post-secondary education. We have always been involved in education as parents, teachers and board members, and we are well aware of the benefits of a good education for the individual and society. Now, we needed to help our children make wise choices for their further education.

We were aware that many of their friends did not have the same kinds of options available to them to attend the more expensive Christian colleges and universities. Thus began our small effort to make Christian post-secondary education a possibility for those who wanted it. But once our eyes are open to the possibilities and needs, we see so much more. Soon, we became aware of many young members of our church community, all deserving of a good education, that could benefit from our help.

So, in 1992, we set up the Oikodome Foundation with an education focus, and in 1993, we received our official approval. Oikodome (*oikos*, a home; *demo*, to build) is a Greek word used in the New Testament; it is commonly translated as "building," or as "edification and building up." We thought it a fitting name, since through Oikodome, we are trying to build up and edify the whole person, so they would be better equipped to edify the whole community.

It has been a guiding general principle that we would support mainly those with whom we had a direct relationship, either as extended family, friends, fellow church or school community members, employees' families, etc. We chose this direction because we feel that it is important to do more than write cheques. We enjoy being able to personally encourage the recipients, watch them grow in their journeys, and see some of the benefits enrich our churches and communities. Also, this way, we limit the applicants to a manageable number. We began by providing the difference between the public universities and TWU's tuition. With the input of the recipients, when we had many more applicants than we could fund at this level, we went from a standard difference payment to making individual assessments based on need. This method is more subjective, and therefore, easier to make when you are familiar with the families.

As time went on and we could afford to invest more dollars into the Foundation, we have moved more and more to supporting some schools' tuition assistance programs directly, relying on them to make recommendations and do the necessary due diligence.

Living in the midst of the brokenness and pain of our world, we see God's grace shine through in the hearts and dreams of many who are gifted with the passion and gifts to be vessels of God's love and wisdom, instruments of his justice, and peace. It is our hope that by providing tuition assistance, we play a small part in building a new generation of focused, well equipped, energetic people who will bring a new energy and vision into our churches, hospitals, schools, businesses, governments, mission fields, etc.

In 2000, we expanded our partnership with Trinity Western University (TWU) by establishing the Geneva Chair of Worldview Studies to enrich TWU's evangelical base with a Reformed voice. The first person to occupy that chair was Dr. Hans Boersma, our former pastor. He later left to take on the J. I. Packer Chair of Theology at Regent College and was replaced by Dr. Mike Goheen. Fourteen years after we established the Chair, Dr. Goheen, decided to go elsewhere, and for various reasons, we didn't replace him, deciding to leave the chair vacant.

A few years later, the University of the Fraser Valley (UFV) approached us, asking whether we would be willing to sponsor a chair in Peace and Conflict Studies there. This idea had morphed out of their Mennonite Faith and Learning Society Chair, which was not achieving the student interest required to sustain the program. Various UFV centres and faculties had gotten together to envision such a degree-granting program.

We agreed that we would provide partial funding for five years, hoping that we could attract more and varied support.

The program successfully launched and was self-sustaining within three years, so we agreed to allocate the rest of the funds toward establishing a Peace and Reconciliation Centre as a community–university partnership. Once again, it was so important for me to be able to speak my faith and passion in the language of the broader community. I've learned so much about peace building, transforming conflict, and being healers by supporting and working toward reconciliation. As Christians, we think we have, and should have, a pretty good idea of how to be peace builders. Yet, when we broaden the conversation, including people from various and no faith backgrounds, there is such an explosion of understanding and potential.

Oikodome is a channel for our family members to be involved in and promote philanthropy. We try to keep it very real by encouraging family members to bring needs they are aware of and care about, whether that's a friend needing a bursary or an organization they are involved with, or just something they believe in. This has resulted in some very interesting projects to support.

The Foundry is a collaboration and integration of health and support services for twelve- to twenty-four-year-olds; it is a wraparound, one-stop agency. The Foundry consists of fourteen different agencies, including Government health and youth agencies and some other local initiatives that work cooperatively to provide this support to our youth and their families in creative and connected ways. Archway Community Services (formerly known as Abbotsford Community Services before they rebranded) provided the leadership and oversight, but they needed some funding to be able to get it established.

Abbotsford's Foundry was one of the first expansions of the successful Vancouver pilot project, and since then, many more locations have opened across British Columbia.

My son-in-law, Jake, was a passionate supporter and member of the Board of Directors of the Wellspring Foundation. This fantastic, visionary initiative of some of his TWU fellow students is bringing peace and hope to Rwanda by providing high-quality, visionary teacher education and support.

Elsa and her husband, Derek, met at Timberline Ranch and are enthusiastic and active supporters of their projects. Many other family members have fond memories of the Ranch's summer camps, and they learned valuable leadership skills when attending them. When it became more challenging for Timberline to attract older and more experienced volunteers because they needed to be earning money for their post-secondary education, Oikodome helped them set up a bursary program for college-and university-bound young people.

Ben (now "Benji" after a seven-year stint living in Sydney, Australia after graduating from TWU) came back home and picked up some of the threads of his teen years. An old high school friend, Chad, was now a youth worker with Youth Unlimited. Chad, Benji, and a number of other friends had spent hours fixing up project cars in our garage in their teens. They not only enjoyed and learned from those experiences, but they also knew that this was a very good way to build relationships among teens—taking apart cars, figuring out how it all works, putting it back together, and then celebrating by taking it out for a spin or to the racetrack.

Chad knows and loves cars. He also has a big heart for the many young men who grow up in apartments, often fatherless, with no one to teach them the confidence-building and employable skills. But he knows that once you can reach these young men and help them build some self-confidence and skills, you also have an open heart to teach and mentor important values and help them launch more successful relationships and careers.

Thus, the Shop Project was born. They began in a Surrey High School, using their shop after hours. With COVID-19 shutting down or limiting many programs, they soon found a new facility, equipped it with basic tools, some project cars, bikes, etc., and they branded it as Young Guns Garage. Soon, they were off and running. The project is still in its infancy at the time of writing, but Benji, Chad, and a whole team of other enthusiasts have big dreams for it as it "grows up." I love to hear the stories of teens who come in with no confidence and are soon opening up and flourishing.

Oikodome marked its twenty-fifth anniversary by looking back and celebrating the many people it has invested in over the years. There are about three hundred beneficiaries that are now serving as doctors, lawyers, teachers, businesspeople, social workers, pastors, counsellors, actors, artists, musicians, community leaders, and in so many other ways. I'm so proud of all of them, and I am thankful that Oikodome has had a small part in helping them reach their goals. When we meet the students for a casual lunch, I will often tell them, "Please know that, besides your own family and friends, there are many people, even strangers, who believe in you and want to support you and invest in your growth."

Now, Oikodome is looking forward. Our past has given us valuable principles of investing in people, their dreams, and their projects. We believe in staying personally connected, working together with others in partnership, and being visionary. Our future will potentially take us through new doors and into exciting opportunities.

# CHAPTER 34

## Business Again

One might have thought that we were done with business when we sold the operating companies to our sons and the holding company to all our children. But no—God, it seems, is not done with us yet. After all, God has invested a substantial bit of experience and knowledge in the two of us, and there are yet many opportunities.

Vanderpol's Eggs began in the early 1950s by selling eggs door to door. They soon expanded to serving corner stores and restaurants. Salvaging cracked and broken eggs with the philosophy of "waste not, want not," we started selling to bakeries. This eventually led to a full-scale further processing plant, where we opened the shells and separated the yolks and whites to sell as separate products. We also created ready-to-use liquid and frozen whole eggs products for restaurants and food manufacturing markets.

In the 1980s, we began taking it to the next step by extracting lysozyme from the egg whites. At this time, we became much more aware of, and amazed by, the miracle of the egg and the wealth stored within that shell. This dive into the inner potential of the egg also expanded us outward toward international and more diverse markets.

For the last fifteen years or so, we have been actively investigating the mysteries and under-explored powers locked within the egg yolk while deepening our awareness of global needs and uses.

It's an apt metaphor for our lives. We start as children by taking things at face value, like an egg in its shell. Then, in adolescence or young adulthood, we crack the shell, our safe and simple beliefs, to examine the details more closely, while also expanding our circle outward. We know it needs to be done with care, but we learn to better understand the beliefs and practices we have held for so long. With better understanding, we can begin to work with and apply these principles in new ways. So, we create or adapt new principles and systems to live by, and they better equip us to live our lives as parents and leaders. When we continue the path of deeper thinking—of asking questions, exploring options, observing and building relationships with other explorers—we continually unlock life's secrets and deeper truths.

We are now at the stage where we can take apart the yolk into its various components and work with each isolate to release and maximize its goodness. The components, working alone or in unique compounds, have the potential to help create a healthier society by reducing our dependence on potentially harmful chemicals and creating new possibilities for healthy living. We are continuously amazed by the very powerful healing powers of the egg that need focused processing so we can extract and maximize their use. So it is with our relationship with God and our understanding of the Bible.

A friend of ours, who was a part of the group of companies twenty years ago, saw the potential for isolating some of these bounties. However, research, product development, and marketing costs were high. Pieter and I recognized and applauded his passion and supported him through various attempts, but each time the projects went sideways.

Then came 2020. Our team of five have been amazed so often. All the things that just wouldn't come together before seemed to slide into place: proven technology, interested customers, global partners, a facility and strategic people (including employees), contractors, and connections. There's little chance we would have found these people and opportunities on our own. So, as we delved further inward, into the mysteries of the egg, and outward, to better defined global needs, we were also delving into the mysteries of divine love, direction, and its global impact.

Yes, there are plenty of real-time problems to be solved, hard work to be done, risks to be taken, and sacrifices to be made to remind us that we are a very necessary part of this story. And then there's the mystery. Why didn't this happen the first, second, or third time he tried to build this business? Why did it take twenty years of effort and faith in the product? And will it actually work this time?

The possibility of success brings up another whole set of questions and opportunities. We could potentially make good profits. And we're also seeing, through Oikodome and community work, how money, wisely and strategically invested and directed, could be used to build a healthier local and global community. I'm waiting to see how this will all come together. I'm pretty sure it will. I have no idea what it will actually look like. Of course, I have some scenarios in mind, but I've learned that it's too easy to think too small, so I'll wait patiently and do my part to live a life of love for this world.

I'm constantly in awe.

# CHAPTER 35

## Peace Keeper or Peace Builder

In the Enneagram personality test, I am a Type 9—a peacemaker. I strive for a peaceful environment and existence, and I avoid conflict as much as I can. I've sometimes defined myself as a "jack of all trades, master of none." That's my gift and strength. I don't ever see myself achieving greatness in any particular thing because there are so many others with greater gifts that can and will do that. But I have enough traces of the different types to allow me to understand, empathize, and support those with a diversity of abilities and character.

I'm a big-picture thinker. When I enter a new place or situation, I need to take time to scan everything, getting a general idea of the lay of the land before my eyes can begin to settle on specifics. When presented with a 'problem' or question, my mind automatically does a wide "Google search" to at least be aware of as many potential possibilities as I can. It drives my husband crazy because he's a problem solver who will first look through the mental catalogue of his experiences to find an "already purchased and proven" solution that can be repurposed. I frustrate him by complicating everything with all of my "we coulds," and he pushes me to pick one (or two) so I can move forward. Together, we can eventually make it work for good.

I'm a connector. Maybe it harks back to, or was honed by, my teaching experiences, where I intentionally tried to integrate learning to connect the various siloed subject categories and make it meaningful in our context. Or maybe it's being the fifth child of eight. I love to observe and explore the interconnectedness of relationships, events, and knowledge. It's satisfying to be able to connect people to people and explore the synergies of their ideas. Community life tends to be very siloed. Each organization operates with its own vision, mission, values, and strategic plan. While they are doing great and very important things, they are often reinventing the wheel, duplicating efforts, or operating with a narrower than necessary perspective and skill set. And then there are the gaps that no one pays attention to until its too late.

I love to host and extend hospitality and provide a welcoming place for family, friends, and community members. Happiness to me is making a pot of soup to share or pouring a coffee or a glass of wine to sit down for a homey chat or stimulating discussion. When that room is filled with people from various positions, ages, and backgrounds, with a common desire to make something better, beautiful things can and do happen.

Now that I'm in my seventies, drawing on a lifetime of such varied experiences, I'm still very much enjoying opportunities to learn, connect, and build peace. I want to be more than a peacemaker, a conflict tamer, or avoider. I want to be a peace builder. We can find ways, from small, everyday, encouraging, healing words and actions to being a part of designing or building visionary projects that will prevent and heal brokenness and trauma. We, as a society, can learn how to use conflict, differing visions, wants, and needs in respectful ways to create more win/win situations where we are all better off.

It can only really be accomplished when each one of us desires to live our stories thoughtfully and intentionally, with care and respect for our world and each and every person and creature. That has as much to do with letting go of the noise and clutter of our world as it has with thoughtfully exploring and enjoying the gifts of each day. As we grow, learn, and become ourselves, we will influence and change the culture, systems, and structures of our society from deep within.

I'm ready to move on from this viewpoint and continue the journey with a renewed sense of hope and comfort. One last look back, the clouds lift, and a sunbeam lights up other mountains and valleys going off to the horizon that I have not personally travelled. It reminds me that my story is the legacy of the stories of the people that have come before. My grandparents and ancestors lived their truths in their times, leaving their legacy in their stories. My parents, family, teachers, pastors, friends, and mentors have influenced my story. My life will be a part of the stories of those of you who walk with me now and who will carry on after my time here is done.

Some Indigenous communities have a practice, which the local Sto:lo people call *tomiyeqw*: Seven Generations back and Seven Generations forward. They live in community with their past and the future. The tried and tested values and truths learned and held by their people, going back seven generations, guide them as they make their decisions on the issues of the day, recognizing that these decisions and actions will affect the next seven generations. They understand that they inherit a wisdom from the past, as well as a duty and responsibility that goes far beyond their day-to-day existence. When I first heard about this, it rang so true.

I, too, am surrounded by a great cloud of witnesses to life's truths in my ancestral line, my faith inheritance, and my culture. As I live my everyday life in this pivotal time—at the end and the beginning of a millennium—it is my turn and responsibility to interpret the times, to take the opportunities to preserve what is good and to build better for those who come after me. As society continues to learn and grow, whether it is in technology, sciences, history, theology, or any other area, we must use the plumb line of these ancient truths of love, justice, mercy, and kindness to know how to best live with them.

So, dear reader, I wish to leave you with peace and hope. Most of our days seem insignificant. Some of them feel like a disaster. Yet, when we step back and observe from an available viewpoint, we see the trends and patterns. We see the roles other people played, the choices we made, and how it affected who we are and how we live today. Yes, we can and must choose whether to dwell on that which hurt and held us back, or the people, choices, and events that give us hope and strength. Our life is what it is. We can't go back and change the past. We also can't change other people. However, we can choose who we want to be and what we can do today.

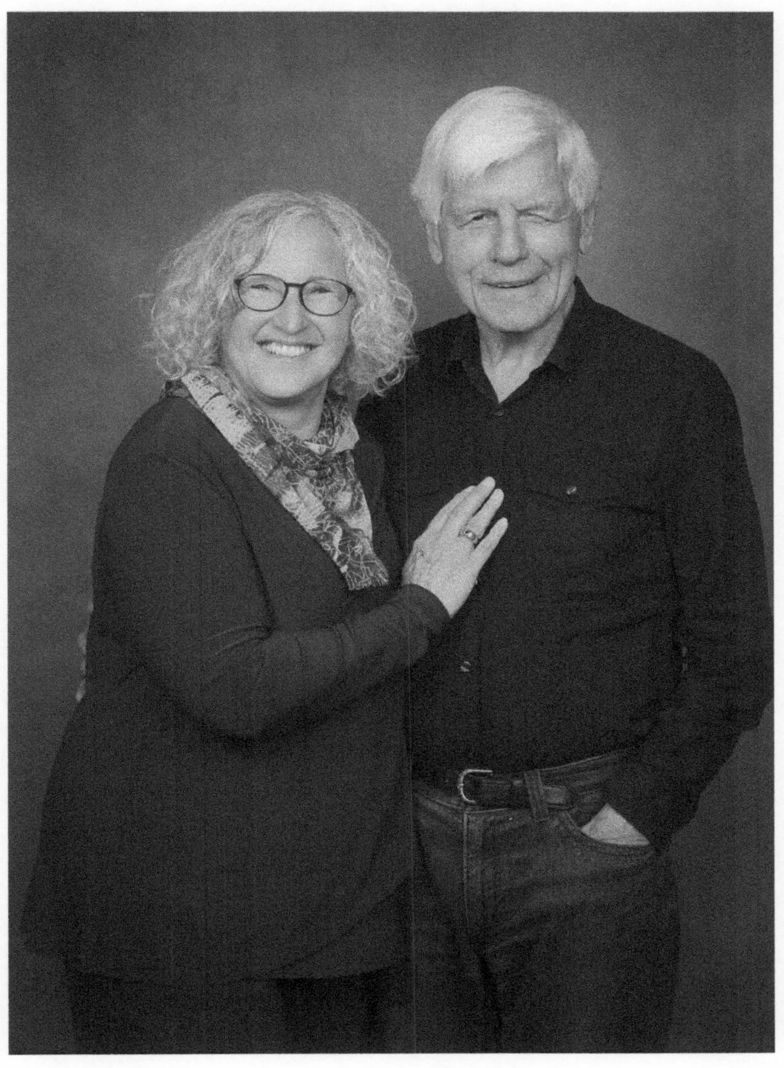

*Thank you for journeying with us*

Fran Vanderpol immigrated to Canada as an infant and grew up in southern Ontario. She taught elementary school for 14 yrs. there and then moved to Beautiful BC to marry Pieter, a widower with six children. They added six more children and now have 27 grandchildren and 3 great grandchildren. Yes, family celebrations are very prized!

Together with Pieter they have been involved in the world of business, philanthropy, church and community building.

She and Pieter live in Abbotsford, BC, They share a house with one of their daughters, son-in-law, and their young family. All of their twelve children live in Southwestern BC.